"I have been waiting for this book. Randall Balmer's *Bad Faith* is the essential reader for all who want to know how America was pushed to the brink and how the evangelical church was led off a cliff. Balmer's *Bad Faith* tells the story of how white supremacy was, and continues to be, the central motivating factor of the Religious Right—not abortion. This quick and easy read packs a mighty punch. Every American must read this book before they cast their next vote."

— **Lisa Sharon Harper**
author of *The Very Good Gospel*

"This brilliant, readable detective story demonstrates that the Religious Right, far from speaking for all evangelicals, has masked its recent—and deviant—origin among groups advocating white supremacy. Here Randall Balmer, our most influential historian of American evangelical Christianity, sets forth the evidence and calls for evangelical Christians to return to their actual sources—the teachings of Jesus."

— **Elaine Pagels**
Harrington Spear Paine Professor of Religion
at Princeton University

"*Bad Faith* is a fantastic primer on one of the most potent and controversial political forces of the past half century—the Religious Right. *Bad Faith* upends the tidy narrative that protesting abortion was the issue that rallied evangelicals in the political realm. Randall Balmer's historical research helps restore the true and infuriating story, that racism, once again, played a central role in shaping the political and religious landscape of the nation. Before you read another headline or write another social media post about religion, race, or politics, read this book."

— **Jemar Tisby**
New York Times bestselling author of *The Color of Compromise: The Truth about the American Church's Complicity in Racism*

"This compelling, timely, tremendously important book is nothing less than the definitive origin story of the Religious Right. Balmer performs an essential service in definitively debunking the myth that the Religious Right was originally organized around opposition to abortion. The revealing and damning truth is that the Religious Right was initially organized in opposition to desegregating private Christian schools, which confirms that the Religious Right has always been racialized in its tactics and political aims. Their most recent embrace of Trumpism and all it represents is therefore the fruit of a poisonous tree of white supremacy and the Religious Right's racial grievance politics nearly half a century in the making. You simply must read this book."

— **Jim Wallis**
New York Times bestselling author of *Christ in Crisis?
Reclaiming Jesus in a Time of Fear, Hate, and Violence*

"In spare and elegant prose, Balmer demolishes the myth that abortion was the issue that launched the Religious Right and replaces it with uncomfortable fact: it was always about race. More than that, Balmer asks us to consider the consequences of the later suppression of that fact, and points to a profound connection between that willful forgetting and the alliance of the Religious Right with white supremacy and racist demagoguery today. *Bad Faith* invites us all to rethink our assumptions about the nexus of race, religion, and politics and the origins of our present crisis."

— **Katherine Stewart**
author of *The Power Worshippers:
Inside the Dangerous Rise of Religious Nationalism*

"It is time evangelicals are better understood. They matter. Trump. Need I say more? As someone who helped contribute to fomenting the lie-based Republican strategy of a 'pro-life' platform back in the 1970s and '80s, and who has heartily repented of my and my father Francis Schaeffer's part in making abortion the divisive 'litmus test' it became, it is a relief to read the hard unvarnished and unlovely truth Balmer exposes in *Bad Faith*. America has paid dearly for the incursion of far-right evangelicals into her politics. The word *timely* hardly covers it in describing Balmer's book. Anyone who wants to find the way back from the evangelical/Republican suicide pact of the Trump years needs to read this book."

— **Frank Schaeffer**
author of *Crazy for God: How I Grew Up as One of the Elect, Helped Found the Religious Right, and Lived to Take All (or Almost All) of It Back*

Bad Faith

Race and the Rise of the Religious Right

Randall Balmer

WILLIAM B. EERDMANS PUBLISHING COMPANY

GRAND RAPIDS, MICHIGAN

Wm. B. Eerdmans Publishing Co.
4035 Park East Court SE, Grand Rapids, Michigan 49546
www.eerdmans.com

27 26 25 24 23 22 21   1 2 3 4 5 6 7

ISBN 978-0-8028-7934-9

Library of Congress Cataloging-in-Publication Data

Names: Balmer, Randall Herbert, author.
Title: Bad faith : race and the rise of the religious right / Randall
    Balmer.
Description: Grand Rapids, Michigan : William B. Eerdmans
    Publishing Company, 2021. | Includes bibliographical
    references and index. |
Summary: "A history of the origins of the Religious Right
    that challenges the commonly held misconception that
    abortion was its original galvanizing issue"—Provided by
    publisher.
Identifiers: LCCN 2020056557 | ISBN 9780802879349
    (hardcover)
Subjects: LCSH: Religious right—United States—History. |
    Evangelicalism—Political aspects—United States—History.
    | Abortion—Political aspects—United States—History. |
    Racism—United States—Religious aspects.
Classification: LCC BR1642.U5 B338 2021 |
    DDC 277.3/0825—dc23
LC record available at https://lccn.loc.gov/2020056557

I don't want to see religious bigotry in any form. It would disturb me if there was a wedding between the religious fundamentalists and the political right. The hard right has no interest in religion except to manipulate it.

—Billy Graham,
Parade Magazine, 1981

Contents

CONTENTS

Part Three: So What?

Preface

In 1990, I was invited to a closed-door conference in Washington, DC, marking the tenth anniversary of Ronald Reagan's election to the presidency. I wasn't sure then why I was included, although I now suspect it was because the previous year I had published a book about American evangelicalism, *Mine Eyes Have Seen the Glory: A Journey into the Evangelical Subculture in America*. I recall debating at the last minute whether or not to attend the event in Washington; the crush of teaching and tending to a young family prompted me to reconsider whether I would accept the invitation.

I decided to go, and it turns out that gathering in a small conference room in many ways redirected the course of my scholarship. In addition to fellow historians George Marsden and Grant Wacker, I found myself in a room with such luminaries of the Religious Right as Paul Weyrich, head of the Free Congress Foundation; Richard Viguerie, direct-mail mogul for conservative causes; Donald Wildmon, founder of the American Family Association; Ralph Reed, executive director of the Christian Coalition; Richard Land, head of the Ethics & Religious Liberty Commission of the Southern Baptist Convention; Carl F. H. Henry, founding editor of *Christianity Today*; and Ed Dobson, one of Jerry Falwell's surrogates in Moral Majority who had since moved on to become pastor of an evangelical megachurch in Grand Rapids, Michigan.

In the course of the opening session, Weyrich, the architect of the Religious Right, embarked on an impassioned soliloquy in which he declared that abortion had nothing whatsoever to do with the emergence of the Religious Right. Dobson quickly concurred.[1]

During the break immediately following the session, I sought out Weyrich to ensure that I had understood him correctly. He was emphatic. He had been trying since the Goldwater campaign in 1964 to mobilize evangelical voters, he said, by raising such issues as school prayer, pornography, the proposed Equal Rights Amendment, and abortion, but nothing galvanized evangelical leaders to action until the Internal Revenue Service began to challenge the tax-exempt status of racially segregated schools.

Although I did not, and do not, care for Weyrich's hard-right politics, his statement sounded plausible. At that point, I had spent most of my life embedded in what I call the evangelical subculture, a vast and interlocking network of churches, denominations, Bible camps, Bible institutes, colleges, seminaries, publishing houses, and mission societies. Specifically, my father was a pastor for forty years in the Evangelical Free Church of America, and I spent my childhood in parsonages in rural southern Minnesota, Michigan, and Iowa. I attended church several times a week, Sunday school, vacation Bible school, and Bible camp; while we lived in Michigan, my father was the driving force behind the formation of Spring Hill Camps, now one of the largest evangelical camps in the nation.

I mention all this only incidentally to establish my evangelical credentials. The real purpose is to say that I don't recall abortion being a topic of conversation in evangelical circles in the middle decades of the twentieth century, so Weyrich's declaration struck me as credible. During the 1970s, the decade when the Religious Right began to emerge, I attended and graduated from an evangelical school, Trinity College in Deerfield, Illinois, and then worked in the development department for its sister institution, Trinity Evangelical Divinity School, while completing a master's degree in church history as a part-time student. As it happens, a single member of the seminary faculty, Harold O. J. Brown, became exercised about abortion, what most evangelicals considered a "Catholic issue," in the latter part of the 1970s. But he was regarded as an outlier, an exception that proved the rule, on a faculty more interested in recondite doctrines such as biblical inerrancy, the notion that the Scriptures are entirely without error in the original (no longer extant) manuscripts.[2]

Weyrich's statement set me on a course to find the true origins of the Religious Right, a quest that took me to the Ford, Carter, and Reagan presidential libraries; the archives at Liberty and Bob Jones universities; and Paul Weyrich's papers at the University of Wyoming in Laramie. I also had several conversations with Frank Schaeffer, who produced a series of antiabortion films called *Whatever Happened to the Human Race?*, which featured his father, Francis A. Schaeffer, and C. Everett Koop.

This book recounts what I discovered.

Definitions and Terms

A number of scholars have tried to make the term "evangelical" more difficult than necessary. "Evangelical," at its root, refers to the Gospels, the first four books of the New Testament, written by the "evangelists": Matthew, Mark, Luke, and John. The term, therefore, connotes the gospel, or good news, of the Bible. Martin Luther's "rediscovery of the gospel" in the sixteenth century gave the term a Protestant cast; Protestant churches in Germany to this day bear the label *Evangelische*.

In North America, evangelicalism emerged from the confluence of what I call the three *P*s in the middle decades of the eighteenth century: the vestiges of New England Puritanism, Scots-Irish Presbyterianism, and Continental Pietism. These strands ignited into a huge conflagration of religious enthusiasm known to historians as the Great Awakening. To this day, evangelicalism in America bears the marks of those initial influences—the obsessive introspection of the Puritans, the doctrinal precision of the Presbyterians, and the emphasis on a warm-hearted, affective spirituality from Pietism.

American evangelicalism was further shaped by a second wave of revivals, which historians unimaginatively call the Second Great Awakening, that occurred roughly from the 1790s through the 1830s. It was during this period that evangelicalism developed an agenda for social reform that in many ways shaped the conscience of the nation.

So what, or who, is an "evangelical"? I prefer a three-part—trinitarian!—definition.

First, an evangelical is someone who believes in the Bible as God's revelation to humanity. She or he is therefore disposed to read it seriously and even to interpret it literally, although evangelicals (like other believers) typically engage in the ruse of selective literalism.

Second, because of their literal reading of the Bible, evangelicals believe in the centrality of conversion, which they derive from the third chapter of the Gospel of John in the New Testament. There, Nicodemus, a Jewish leader, approaches Jesus by night and asks how he can gain entrance into the kingdom of heaven. Jesus replies that he must be "born again" or, in some translations, "born from above." Conversion, for evangelicals, is generally understood as a "turning away" from sin to embrace salvation, and the "born-again" experience is very often (though not always) dramatic and accompanied by considerable emotion. It is also usually a datable experience; most evangelicals will be able to recount the time and the circumstances of their conversions.

Finally, most evangelicals are committed to "evangelism," bringing others into the faith. The biblical warrant for this is what evangelicals recognize as the Great Commission at the end of the Gospel of Mark, where Jesus instructs his followers to "Go into all the world and preach the good news to all creation." Very often, however, rather than do the evangelism themselves, evangelicals hire professionals to do it for them: missionaries, for example, or pastors of outreach or evangelism on the staffs of large churches. Still, most evangelicals will affirm their responsibility to bring others into the faith.

In terms of numbers, survey data suggest that evangelicals make up anywhere from 25 to 46 percent of the population in the United States. A reasonably safe estimate would be that evangelicals comprise one-third of the population.

The movement of politically conservative evangelicals that emerged in the late 1970s has been called many things, including the New Christian Right, the Christian Right, and the Religious Right. I prefer the latter, Religious Right.

As with many such designations, the term is more approximate than it is precise. There is no centralized headquarters for "the Religious Right," no computerized listing of "card-carrying" members. The label is a term of convenience that, much like the word "generation," defies easy definition. I use the term "Religious Right" to denote a movement of politically conservative evangelicals who, since the late 1970s, have sought to exert their influence in political, cultural, and legal matters. Some observers call them fundamentalists, though not all fundamentalists are part of the Religious Right, and the Religious Right includes many other kinds of evangelicals—pentecostals, for instance—besides fundamentalists.[1]

The Religious Right, moreover, consists of conservative evangelicals both individually and collectively, so it would encompass individual believers as well as a myriad of loosely allied organizations that may or may not fully agree with one another.

The term "New Christian Right" has always baffled me because it suggests there was at one time an *Old* Christian Right, and, try as I might as a historian, I've never been able to determine when that was—unless it was the crusty anticommunism of fringe characters like Carl McIntire and Billy James Hargis in the 1940s and 1950s or the stubborn segregationism of the Jim Crow era. But either attribution, I think, demeans the faith. "Christian Right" may be less problematic historically, but I find it objectionable on moral and theological grounds. When I was a child, my mother taught me that whenever anyone asked me about my religion, I should reply, "I don't have a religion; I'm a *Christian*."[2]

As I will argue in the pages that follow, I'm afraid I don't find much that I recognize as *Christian* in the actions and policies of the Religious Right.

PART ONE

*Evangelicalism before
the Religious Right*

1

The Emergence of
Progressive Evangelicalism

The alliance between white evangelicals and the far-right precincts of the Republican Party over the past forty-plus years has been so unwavering that most Americans would be forgiven for believing that evangelicalism has always listed to the right of the political spectrum. That, however, is not the case. Over the course of the nineteenth and well into the twentieth century, evangelicals were engaged in a broad spectrum of social reform efforts, many of them directed toward those on the margins of society.

Aside from the Civil War, the Second Great Awakening was arguably the most consequential event in American history. Coming on the heels of the American Revolution and taking place during the decades straddling the turn of the nineteenth century, the evangelical revivals associated with the Second Awakening convulsed three theaters of the new nation—New England, the Cumberland Valley of Kentucky, and upstate New York—and utterly reshaped religion in America.

The New England phase was relatively placid. The epicenter of the awakening in New England was Yale College, where Timothy Dwight, president of the school and grandson of the redoubtable Jonathan Edwards, succeeded in turning students away from Enlightenment rationalism and toward orthodox Christianity. In 1802, one of those students, Benjamin Silliman, described Yale as a "little temple" where "prayer and praise seem to be the delight of the greater part of the students." The *Connecticut Evangelical Magazine* reported another awakening at Yale in 1815, and Nathaniel William Taylor, pastor of the First Congregational Church in New Haven, witnessed a more general revival in both the school and the town in January 1821. As Yale graduates fanned out to congregations across New England, revivals often followed in places from New York to Maine, from Vermont to Rhode Island.[1]

The Cumberland Valley theater was by far the most dramatic. This is the era of the camp meetings, when settlers gathered for a week or ten days of socializing, hymn singing, prayer, and preaching, which started at sunrise and lasted well into the night. Although critics contended that more souls were conceived than converted, contemporaries tell of people being "slain in the Spirit," which manifested itself in all sorts of "exercises"—barking, jerking uncontrollably, or falling to the ground. As settlers in this frontier area returned to their homes, they organized Baptist congregations and, with the help of circuit riders, Methodist churches, thereby stamping the South with an evangelical, revivalist ethic that persists to this day.[2]

Abetted by the population and economic boom from construction of the Erie Canal, some of the revival energies shifted toward western New York by the late 1820s and early 1830s. The people of Rochester, New York, reported a "powerful revival of religion" as early as April 1827, and the region was so singed by the fires of revival that it became known as the "burned-over district." The arrival of Charles Grandison Finney in Rochester in 1830 gave the revival a boost. "Mr. Finney is preaching to overflowing houses," the *Baptist Chronicle* reported. "Conversions are daily occurring," including "men of wealth, talents, and influence." African Americans also responded to revival preaching. Two "respectable African preachers" arrived in town, according to the *African Repository & Colonial Journal*, and their efforts produced such an evangelical awakening "the like has never been known among the Africans in this place before!"[3]

Finney and other evangelical revivalists in the nineteenth century, however, believed that evangelicalism entailed more than mere conversions. A regenerated individual, in obedience to the teachings of Jesus, bore responsibility for the improvement of society and especially the interests of those most vulnerable. Finney, in fact, understood benevolence toward others as a necessary corollary of faith. "God's rule requires universal benevolence," he wrote. "I abhor a faith which has no humanity in it and with it," he added. "God loves both piety and humanity."[4]

The program of social reform unleashed by Finney and other evangelicals early in the nineteenth century stands in marked contrast to the agenda of the Religious Right. For antebellum evangelicals, benevolence took many forms, including education, prison reform, and advocacy for the poor and for the rights of women. Many evangelicals, seeking to obey the commands of Jesus to love their enemies and turn the other cheek, enlisted in efforts to oppose violence and war; I've even discovered a reference to an evangelical campaign for gun control. Even though the evangelical obsession with temperance looks presumptuous and paternalistic in hindsight, the temperance movement was a response to the very real depredations and suffering, including spousal and child abuse, caused by excessive alcohol consumption.

While it is true that many Southerners, notably James Henley Thornwell and Robert Lewis Dabney, defended slavery, many evangelicals in the North sought to end the scourge of slavery. Some evangelicals were caught up in nativist sentiments, but a far greater number supported such initiatives as public education, known then as common schools, so that the children of immigrants and those less fortunate could toe the ladder of upward mobility. "Common schools are the glory of our land," a writer declared in the *Christian Spectator*, "where even the beggar's child is taught to read, and write, and think, for himself."[5]

From a remove of a couple of centuries, it's tempting to retroject twenty-first-century sensibilities onto these evangelical reformers, and in so doing some of their attitudes and approaches come off as paternalistic and overweening, even colonialist. Nineteenth-century evangelicals didn't always get it right. But it is also true that the Second Awakening energized an extraordinary mobilization of evangelicals on behalf of those Jesus called "the least of these." Animated by their desire to bring about the kingdom of God on earth, they sought to alleviate suffering and work toward equality—crudely and imperfectly at times, to be sure, but determinedly. Theirs was not an abstract faith. Antebellum evangelicals understood that, in Finney's words, "God loves both piety and humanity."

The Diversion of Dispensationalism

In the decades following the Second Great Awakening, early in the nineteenth century, evangelicals plunged into the enterprise of social reform, including common schools, peace crusades, the abolition of slavery, temperance, prison reform, and women's rights. What animated their efforts was the conviction that they could reform society according to the norms of godliness and thereby bring about the kingdom of God here on earth—and, more particularly, here in America.

Theologians call this *postmillennialism*, the doctrine that Jesus will return to earth *after* the millennium, the thousand-year period of peace and righteousness predicted in the book of Revelation. The corollary was that it was incumbent on the faithful to reform society and pave the way for the "second coming" of Jesus.

Those efforts at social reform were remarkably fruitful. Evangelicals succeeded in shaping the conscience of the nation in the early decades of the nineteenth century, and their persistence eventually drove an angry South to secession. But the Civil War itself began to prompt a reconsideration of postmillennialism. The battlefields of Gettysburg and Antietam and Manassas, not to mention the horrific tally of casualties (historians now estimate something close to three-quarters of a million), prompted evangelicals to reexamine their postmillennial optimism about the perfection of society.

The ensuing, postwar decades provided little encouragement. Industrialization and urbanization began to reshape American society. The arrival of non-Protestant immigrants, most of whom did not share evangelical scruples about temperance, came to be seen more as a threat than an opportunity. Teeming, squalid tenements, roiling with labor unrest, hardly resembled the precincts of Zion that evangelicals had so confidently predicted earlier in the century.

Evangelical social reformers encountered the speed bump of apocalypticism beginning in the late nineteenth century and continuing well into the twentieth. Evangelicals began, in greater and greater numbers, to appropriate the ideas of John Nelson Darby, a member of the Brethren (later known as Plymouth Brethren) in Britain. In his writings and during his visits to the United States, Darby informed American evangelicals that they had been interpreting the Bible incorrectly. Jesus would not return to earth *after* the millennium; he would return *before* the millennium, which meant that Christians could anticipate the second coming at any moment, at which time they would be "raptured" into heaven and those "left behind" would face divine judgment.[1]

Darby's interpretive scheme was called *dispensationalism*, or *dispensational premillennialism*, because it divided all of human history into ages, or dispensations. The consequence of Darby's premillennialism (Jesus would return *before* the millennium) was to absolve evangelicals of responsibility for addressing social ills. If Jesus was going to return at any moment, why bother with making this transitory world a better place?

I call premillennialism a theology of despair because it allowed evangelicals to throw up their hands in resignation. At the same time that the Social Gospel began to take hold among Protestant liberals, based on the conviction that God can redeem not only sinful individuals but also sinful social institutions, evangelicals shifted their focus to individual regeneration.

The belief in Christ's imminent return transformed American evangelicalism in ways ranging from trivial to profound. At the former end of that spectrum, premillennialism is responsible for some colossally bad architecture: If Jesus is going to return at any moment, why bother with design or ornamentation? Cinder block will do just fine—the triumph of function over form.

At the other end of the spectrum, premillennialism shifted evangelical attention from the collective ills of society to the salvation of individuals. Premillennialism became a potent device for urging sinners to convert. Preachers would often cajole their congregants into making a profession of faith—what Billy Graham called "making a decision for Christ"—by warning that if they died suddenly or if Jesus returned, as he could at any moment, those who were not "saved" would face judgment and be consigned to hell.

Although premillennialism began to relax its hold on American evangelicals in the 1970s, a motion picture produced in 1972, *A Thief in the Night*, illustrates the power and the persistence of premillennial thought among evangelicals. The movie, written and directed by Donald W. Thompson, opens with a woman awaking from a dream to find her husband's shaver buzzing in the bathroom sink; he has simply disappeared. After the opening music—"I Wish We'd All Been Ready," by Larry Norman—the film continues with some straightforward preaching about the imminent return of Jesus, warning that anyone who is not saved will be damned.[2]

Then Jesus returns, the faithful depart, and those left behind (Tim LaHaye's book and film series by that title were inspired by *A Thief in the Night*) face terrible persecution. Anyone who does not accept the "mark of the beast" is unable to purchase the necessities for survival and is hunted down by the evil authorities. The woman whose husband disappeared in the rapture is pursued by police cars and helicopters. Just as she is about to jump off a dam, she awakens from her dream—and the opening sequence repeats itself. She finds the shaver in the bathroom, searches for her missing husband, and lets out a blood-curdling scream. Jesus has returned to collect the faithful, and she was not ready.

Despite its low budget and some infelicities in acting, *A Thief in the Night* was enormously popular among evangelical audiences. And here, in the interest of full disclosure, I must divulge that Donald Thompson, the writer and director, was my Sunday school teacher. *A Thief in the Night* was inspired by my father's Sunday evening sermons on the book of Revelation at Westchester Evangelical Free Church in Des Moines, Iowa. My father played the "good" preacher in the film, the preacher who warned that Jesus would return at any moment.

The doctrine of dispensational premillennialism—Jesus will return imminently—effectively absolved American evangelicals of responsibility to reform society and redirected their energies toward individual regeneration. With very few exceptions, evangelicals remained outside the political fray in the final decades of the nineteenth century and well into the twentieth.

The Making of the Evangelical Subculture

The month of July 1925 in eastern Tennessee was hot, and nowhere more so than on the second floor of the Rhea County courthouse in Dayton. John Thomas Scopes was on trial for teaching evolution in violation of Tennessee's Butler Act. Scopes, football coach and part-time science teacher, had been recruited by local boosters to test the constitutionality of the law, and even though he couldn't remember whether or not he had actually taught evolution, he agreed to stand trial.[1]

The trial pitted two of the nation's most famous lawyers against one another. Clarence Darrow headed Scopes's defense team, and William Jennings Bryan, three-time Democratic nominee for president and Woodrow Wilson's secretary of state, assisted the prosecution. Journalists flocked to Dayton (as the civic boosters had hoped) to cover the trial; Chicago's WGN radio carried the proceedings live.

A circus atmosphere surrounded the trial, with banners and protesters and monkeys on the court-house lawn. The trial was cast as a contest between science and faith, as a referendum on the veracity of the Bible, especially the Genesis accounts of cre-ation. The irascible and acerbic H. L. Mencken, of the *Baltimore Sun*, no friend of Bryan or his cause, headed the phalanx of journalists. As the trial steam-rolled toward its preordained conclusion that Scopes was guilty, Mencken wrote: "It serves notice on the country that Neanderthal man is organizing in these forlorn backwaters of the land, led by a fanatic, rid of sense and devoid of conscience." Tennessee, he added, "now sees its courts converted into camp meetings and its Bill of Rights made a mock of by its sworn officers of the law."[2]

For their part, America's evangelicals had long felt themselves under siege. The publication of Charles Darwin's *Origin of Species* in 1859 cast doubt on the literal interpretation of Genesis. The discipline of higher criticism, emanating from Ger-many, questioned the authorship of several books of the Bible. For example, how is it, the higher critics asked, that Moses, the putative author of the Pentateuch (the first five books of the Hebrew Bible), records his own death at the end of the book of Deuteronomy?

In addition, the 1920s was the era of jazz and speakeasies and the flapper, women with bobbed hair and short skirts. For many American evangelicals, it seemed as though the larger American culture had turned against them and their values. The Scopes "monkey" trial, as it came to be known, represented the culmination of evangelical uneasiness with the broader society.

Scopes was found guilty of violating the Butler Act and fined $100 (Bryan offered to pay the fine, and the verdict was later overturned on a technicality). But American evangelicals lost decisively in the larger courtroom of public opinion. They were ridiculed, by Mencken and others, as backwoods country bumpkins.

Symbolically, the Scopes trial was a turning point. In the course of the 1920s and 1930s, American evangelicals doubled down on their rejection of the larger culture. Having already embraced premillennialism, the doctrine that Jesus would return to earth at any moment to rain judgment on the unrighteous, evangelicals set about to construct the evangelical subculture, an interlocking network of congregations, denominations, Bible camps, Bible institutes, colleges, seminaries, missionary societies, and publishing houses. The broader culture was both corrupt and corrupting, they argued, and the subculture provided a safe space, a refuge from the dangers of an increasingly secular society.

In the middle decades of the twentieth century, evangelicals sought especially to shield their children from the depredations of that larger world. The subculture served that purpose. It was insular and enveloping, and it was possible (as I can attest personally) to grow up in the evangelical subculture and have very little commerce with anyone outside of that world. Parents could send their children to Sunday school and Bible camp and then to Moody Bible Institute or Multnomah School of the Bible or Westmont College reasonably confident that they would not be corrupted by the outside world.

What were the political ramifications of this retreat into the evangelical subculture? In the short term, during the middle decades of the twentieth century, evangelicals were largely apolitical; they did not participate in politics, certainly not in any organized way. Yes, there were a few evangelicals who made their voices heard—Fighting Bob Shuler, Billy James Hargis, Carl McIntire—but they were fringe characters. Many evangelicals during this time, drawing on their premillennial beliefs and their convictions about the corruptions of American society, refused to register to vote. Politics was the realm of Satan, they reasoned, and besides, this temporal world was condemned and careening toward judgment. Why bother?

But the construction of the evangelical subculture had another, longer-term effect. The time, energy, and money evangelicals invested in their own institutions in the 1920s and 1930s, often starting from scratch, began to reap dividends several decades later. Those institutions, especially schools, evangelistic organizations, and media operations, provided the foundation for evangelicals to reenter the public arena in the 1970s.[3]

4

The Chicago Declaration and
Jimmy Carter

The decade of the 1970s did not begin or end well
for progressive evangelicalism, the tradition ex-
emplified by Charles Grandison Finney and other
nineteenth-century evangelicals. In between the beginning and end of the decade, however, the movement may have reached its zenith with a remarkable
affirmation of evangelical social concern and the
election of a progressive evangelical as president of
the United States.

Richard Nixon's promise of a "secret plan" to
end the war in Vietnam, which boosted him to the
presidency in 1968, turned out to entail expanding
the war to Cambodia in the spring of 1970, thereby
prompting protests across the nation and the shoot-
ing of four students by the Ohio National Guard at
Kent State University on May 4, 1970. Nevertheless,

Nixon rallied his "silent majority" in advance of the 1972 presidential election, and he entered the campaign with decided advantages.

The Democratic nominee was George McGovern, senator from South Dakota, who grew up in the parsonage of a Wesleyan Methodist minister and who himself studied for the ministry at Garrett-Evangelical Theological Seminary before going on to earn the PhD from Northwestern University. McGovern, a decorated war hero in World War II, brought his campaign to Wheaton College's Edman Chapel on the morning of October 11, 1972.

I was a first-year student at Trinity College, and I persuaded several of my classmates to skip our daily chapel and accompany me to Wheaton. I shall never forget the scene. Students paraded around the chapel with Nixon campaign banners. McGovern opened by saying that he had wanted to attend Wheaton, but his family couldn't afford it. He went on to explain that his understanding of justice and social responsibility was derived from the Bible. By the end of his remarks, McGovern had won a respectful hearing from many of the students.

Nevertheless, Billy Graham had endorsed Nixon, and white evangelicals followed the evangelist's lead.

In the course of McGovern's forlorn campaign, however, a small number of evangelicals formed an organization called Evangelicals for McGovern (Richard Mouw, one of the members, joked that the entire caucus could meet in a phone booth). That organization, however, became the basis for a gathering a year later at the Chicago YMCA on Wabash Street. Convened by Ronald J. Sider, fifty-five evangelicals met to hammer out what became known as the Chicago Declaration of Evangelical Social Concern.

The Chicago Declaration was a remarkable document in that it reaffirmed evangelicalism's historical commitment to those Jesus called "the least of these." The declaration decried the persistence of militarism, racism, and economic inequality in American life. It pointed out the scandal of hunger in such an affluent society; it condemned materialism and called for justice. And at the behest of Nancy Hardesty, professor of English at Trinity College, the Chicago Declaration reaffirmed evangelicalism's historic commitment to women's equality.[1]

Within six months, the governor of Georgia addressed a group of graduating seniors at the University of Georgia Law School. He sounded many of the same themes as the Chicago Declaration—racial justice, prison reform, the corruption of regulatory institutions in Washington. Jimmy Carter's extemporaneous remarks were so compelling that one of the journalists in attendance, Hunter S. Thompson of *Rolling Stone*, went to his car to retrieve a tape recorder so he could record something extraordinary, he said later: a politician willing to tell the truth.

In December 1974, Carter announced his candidacy for the Democratic presidential nomination. Carter, a Southern Baptist Sunday school teacher, was unabashed about his faith, repeatedly identifying himself as a "born-again" Christian, thereby sending every journalist in New York to his or her Rolodex to figure out what in the world he was talking about.

At a remove of more than four decades, it is easy to lose sight of the improbability of Carter's ascent to the presidency in the mid-1970s. In November 1974, just before Carter announced his candidacy for the Democratic nomination, Gallup conducted a survey to gauge support for thirty-two potential candidates for president of the United States; Carter's name was not among them. The governor of Georgia determinedly headed for the small towns of New Hampshire and the precincts of Iowa. "Jimmy

Who?" worked harder than anyone else. "I can will myself to sleep until ten-thirty and get my ass beat," he told a relative, "or I can will myself to get up at six o'clock and become President of the United States." His rivals took notice. "Seems like everywhere I've been lately, they tell me Jimmy Carter was just through there a week or so ago," Morris Udall, one of Carter's rivals for the Democratic nomination, complained. "The sonofabitch is as ubiquitous as the sunshine."[2]

On January 19, 1976, Carter finished first in the Iowa precinct caucuses, and he won the New Hampshire primary on February 24. Soon his campaign began to resemble a juggernaut. In Florida, Carter scored his most important, but underappreciated, victory when he dispatched a fellow southern governor. Carter's win on March 9 effectively ended the political career of one of the nation's most notorious segregationists, George C. Wallace of Alabama.

Having secured the Democratic nomination in July, Carter cruised into the general election with what was shaping up as a landslide victory over Gerald R. Ford. Carter's carefully calibrated campaign, however, very nearly imploded over a miscalculation by the candidate. On October 14, just weeks before the election, *Playboy* magazine hit the newsstands. Carter had intended that his interview would dispel any notion of smug self-righteousness on his part, but the media picked up on his statement about lusting after women other than his wife. For evangelicals, that statement was utterly unremarkable—let us remember Jesus's words in the Sermon on the Mount—although a fellow Southern Baptist, picking up on another quote from the interview, allowed that, "well, 'screw' is just not a good Baptist word." The media had a field day. One editorial cartoon depicted the Democratic nominee staring at the Statue of Liberty in a state of undress, and Carter dropped fifteen percentage points in the polls.[3]

Ford, Nixon's appointed successor and Carter's Republican opponent, made a case for his own evangelical credentials. Ford had served on the vestry of his Episcopal parish, and his son Michael was a student at Gordon-Conwell Theological Seminary. For America's evangelicals, however, Carter's "born-again" proclamations were compelling. At a time when they were not organized politically, many evangelicals voted for Carter. Some responded to his promise never knowingly to lie to the American people, a radical idea in the wake of Nixon's endless prevarications. Others embraced his policies. Still others supported Carter out of the sheer novelty of voting for one of their own.

As president, Carter quickly embarked on his agenda. He pardoned Vietnam-era draft evaders, and recognizing that the United States must abandon colonialism if it were to have meaningful relationships with Latin American countries, Carter pursued ratification of the Panama Canal treaties, a process set in motion by Lyndon Johnson. He made peace in the Middle East a priority, which culminated in the historic Camp David Accords. He sought to reorient American foreign policy away from Cold War dualism toward an emphasis on human rights, and he recognized the necessity of conservation and setting the nation on a course toward energy independence. With his protection of wilderness areas, many environmentalists regard Carter as the greatest environmental president ever. He appointed more women and minorities to government posts than any previous president.

Carter's policy ambitions, however, were shackled by a persistently balky economy. Interest rates remained stubbornly high, and the taking of American hostages in Iran in November 1979 cast a pall over his presidency.

What Carter did not know until well into his re-election campaign is that a group of evangelicals had been conspiring against him for some time.

PART TWO

The Abortion Myth and the Rise of the Religious Right

The Abortion Myth

The Religious Right's most cherished and durable myth is its myth of origins. According to this well-rehearsed narrative, articulated by Jerry Falwell, Pat Robertson, and countless others, evangelical leaders were shaken out of their political complacency by the United States Supreme Court's *Roe v. Wade* decision of January 22, 1973. Falwell even recounted, albeit fourteen years later, his horror at reading the news in the January 23, 1973, edition of the *Lynchburg News*. "The Supreme Court had just made a decision by a seven-to-two margin that would legalize the killing of millions of unborn children," Falwell wrote. "I sat there staring at the *Roe v. Wade* story growing more and more fearful of the consequences of the Supreme Court's act and wondering why so few voices had been raised against it." This myth of origins has Falwell and other evangelical leaders emerging like mollusks out of their apolit-ical stupor to fight the moral outrage of legalized abortion. Some even went so far as to invoke the moniker "new abolitionists" in an apparent effort to ally themselves with their antebellum evangelical predecessors who sought to eradicate the scourge of slavery.[1]

The rhetoric about abortion being the catalyst for the rise of the Religious Right, however, col-lapses under scrutiny. Evangelicals considered abortion a "Catholic issue" until the late 1970s. In 1968, the flagship evangelical magazine *Christianity Today* convened a conference with another evan-gelical organization, Christian Medical Society, to discuss the ethics of abortion. After several days of deliberations, twenty-six evangelical theologians issued a statement acknowledging that they could not agree on any one position, that the ambiguities of the issue allowed for many different approaches. "Whether the performance of an induced abortion is sinful we are not agreed," the statement read, "but about the necessity of it and permissibility for it un-der certain circumstances we are in accord." The statement cited "individual health, family welfare, and social responsibility" as possible justifications for abortion and allowed for instances when fetal life "may have to be abandoned to maintain full and secure family life."[2]

Evangelicals in the late 1960s and throughout most of the 1970s by and large refused to see abortion as a defining issue, much less a matter that would summon them to the front lines of political activism. Abortion simply failed to gain traction among evangelicals, and some groups with historic ties to evangelicalism pushed for legalization. In 1970, for example, the United Methodist Church General Conference called on state legislatures to repeal laws restricting abortion, and in 1972, at a gathering Jimmy Carter addressed while governor of Georgia, the Methodists acknowledged "the sanctity of unborn human life" but also declared that "we are equally bound to respect the sacredness of the life and well-being of the mother, for whom devastating damage may result from unacceptable pregnancy."[3]

Meeting in St. Louis, Missouri, during the summer of 1971, the messengers (delegates) to the Southern Baptist Convention passed a resolution that stated, "we call upon Southern Baptists to work for legislation that will allow the possibility of abortion under such conditions as rape, incest, clear evidence of severe fetal deformity, and carefully ascertained evidence of the likelihood of damage to the emotional, mental, and physical health of the mother." The Southern Baptist Convention, hardly a redoubt of liberalism, reaffirmed that position in 1974, the year after the *Roe* decision, and again in 1976.[4]

When the *Roe* decision was handed down on January 22, 1973, W. A. Criswell, former president of the Southern Baptist Convention and pastor of First Baptist Church in Dallas, Texas, expressed his satisfaction with the ruling. "I have always felt that it was only after a child was born and had a life separate from its mother that it became an individual person," one of the most famous fundamentalists of the twentieth century declared, "and it has always, therefore, seemed to me that what is best for the mother and for the future should be allowed."[5]

Baptists, in particular, applauded the *Roe* decision as an appropriate articulation of the line of division between church and state, between personal morality and state regulation of individual behavior. "Religious liberty, human equality and justice are advanced by the Supreme Court abortion decision," W. Barry Garrett of *Baptist Press* wrote. Floyd Robertson of the National Association of Evangelicals disagreed with the *Roe* decision, but he believed that legal redress should not be a priority for evangelicals. "The abortion issue should also remind evangelicals that the church must never rely on the state to support its mission or enforce its moral standards," he wrote in the summer 1973 issue of the organization's newsletter, *United Evangelical Action*. "The church and state must be separate. The actions and conduct of Christians transcend the secular community for which the state is responsible."[6]

A few evangelical voices, including *Christianity Today*, questioned the ruling, although the magazine published an editorial three years later entitled "Is Abortion a Catholic Issue?" That editorial affirmed the general principle of right to life but concluded: "There are, of course, other considerations, such as the rights of the parents and the much-debated question of when life begins."[7]

The overwhelming response to *Roe v. Wade* on the part of evangelicals was silence, and the voices that spoke on the matter were ambivalent. Two successive editors of *Christianity Today*, Carl F. H. Henry and Harold Lindsell, equivocated on abortion. Henry affirmed that "a woman's body is not the domain and property of others"; Lindsell allowed that, "if there are compelling psychiatric reasons from a Christian point of view, mercy and prudence may favor a therapeutic abortion." Even James Dobson, who later became an implacable foe of abortion, acknowledged in 1973 that the Bible was silent on the matter and therefore it was plausible for an evangelical to believe that "a developing embryo or fetus was not regarded as a full human being."[8]

In 1977, another voice, one well respected in evangelical circles, joined the conversation. Introducing himself as "a Christian, as a father, as a minister of the gospel, and as a professor of theology," Walter Martin, a Baptist minister, founder of the Christian Research Institute, and longtime columnist for *Eternity* magazine, took on the issue in a small book entitled *Abortion: Is It Always Murder?* Martin determined that abortion was impermissible as a form of contraception, but he added that it should be allowed in cases of rape and incest or to protect the health of the mother. "I think the people who are against abortion in any form have presumed to instruct the Deity," Martin wrote. "But you cannot say that abortion is always murder." He allowed that Christians were entitled to challenge the law of the land—"It is better to obey God than men"—but he concluded, "We need for God's sake to stop making dogmatic declarations in every area of abortion."[9]

Opposition to abortion was slow to take hold among evangelicals. Falwell issued no public statement on abortion until 1975 and, by his own admission, did not preach against abortion until February 26, 1978, more than five years after the *Roe v. Wade* decision. In 2011, an early antiabortion activist reflected on his reception among evangelicals in the 1970s. "While we evangelicals were dithering," Robert Case recalled, "the Roman Catholics were bearing the torch of salvation for America's unborn." He described his "lukewarm" reception at a meeting of the Evangelical Theological Society and lamented, "Here we were four years after *Roe v. Wade* and evangelical Christians were still ambivalent about abortion."[10]

Despite the persistence of the abortion myth, endlessly propagated by leaders of the Religious Right, evangelicals considered abortion a "Catholic issue" until the late 1970s, and even then, opposition to abortion was slow to take hold.

What Really Happened

The real catalyst for the Religious Right was a court decision, but it was not *Roe v. Wade*. It was a lower court ruling in the District Court for the District of Columbia in a case called *Green v. Connally*. On June 30, 1971, the court ruled that any organization that engaged in racial segregation or racial discrimination was not by definition a charitable institution, and therefore it had no claims on tax-exempt status. The Supreme Court's *Coit v. Green* decision upheld the district court, and the Internal Revenue Service then began making inquiries about the racial policies of so-called segregation academies as well as the fundamentalist school Bob Jones University, in Greenville, South Carolina, which boasted a long history of racial exclusion.

In May 1969, a group of African American parents in Holmes County, Mississippi, led by William H. Green, had sued the secretary of the treasury and the commissioner of the Internal Revenue Service to prevent three new whites-only K-12 private academies from securing tax-exempt status, arguing that their discriminatory policies prevented them from being considered "charitable" institutions. The schools had been founded in the mid-1960s in response to the desegregation of public schools set in motion by the *Brown v. Board of Education* decision of 1954. In 1969, the first year of desegregation, the number of white students enrolled in public schools in Holmes County dropped from 771 to 28; the following year, that number fell to zero.[1]

In *Green v. Kennedy* (David Kennedy was secretary of the treasury at the time), decided in January 1970, the plaintiffs won a preliminary injunction, which denied the "segregation academies" tax-exempt status until further review. In the meantime, the government was solidifying its position on such schools. Later that year, the president, Richard Nixon, ordered the Internal Revenue Service to enact a new policy denying tax exemptions to all segregated schools in the United States. Under the provisions of Title VI of the Civil Rights Act, which forbade racial segregation and discrimination, discriminatory schools were not—by definition—"charitable" educational organizations, and therefore they had no claims to tax-exempt status; similarly, donations to such organizations would no longer qualify as tax-deductible contributions.[2]

On June 30, 1971, the United States District Court for the District of Columbia issued its ruling in the case, now *Green v. Connally* (John Connally had replaced David Kennedy as secretary of the treasury). The decision upheld the new IRS policy: "Under the Internal Revenue Code, properly construed, racially discriminatory private schools are not entitled to the Federal tax exemption provided for charitable, educational institutions, and persons making gifts to such schools are not entitled to the deductions provided in case of gifts to charitable, educational institutions."[3]

Paul Weyrich saw his opening. In the decades following World War II, evangelicals, especially white evangelicals in the North, had drifted toward the Republican Party—inclined in that direction by general Cold War anxieties, vestigial suspicions of Catholicism, and well-known evangelist Billy Graham's very public friendship with Dwight Eisenhower and Richard Nixon. Despite these predilections, though, evangelicals had largely stayed out of the political arena, at least in any organized way. If he could change that, Weyrich reasoned, their large numbers would constitute a formidable voting bloc—one he believed he could marshal behind conservative causes.

"The new political philosophy must be defined by us [conservatives] in moral terms, packaged in non-religious language, and propagated throughout the country by our new coalition," Weyrich wrote in the mid-1970s. "When political power is achieved, the moral majority will have the opportunity to re-create this great nation." Weyrich believed that the political possibilities of such a coalition were unlimited. "The leadership, moral philosophy, and workable vehicle are at hand just waiting to be blended and activated," he wrote. "If the moral majority acts, results could well exceed our wildest dreams."[4]

But this hypothetical "moral majority" (lower-case letters) needed a catalyst, a standard around which to rally. For nearly two decades, Weyrich, by his own account, had been trying out different issues, hoping one might pique evangelical interest: pornography, prayer in schools, the proposed Equal Rights Amendment to the Constitution, even abortion. "I was trying to get these people interested in those issues and I utterly failed," Weyrich recalled in 1990.[5]

The *Green v. Connally* ruling provided a necessary first step: It captured the attention of evangelical leaders, especially as the IRS began sending questionnaires to church-related "segregation academies," including Falwell's own Lynchburg Christian School, inquiring about their racial policies. Falwell was furious. "In some states," he famously groused, "it's easier to open a massage parlor than a Christian school."[6]

One such school, Bob Jones University, a fundamentalist college in Greenville, South Carolina, was especially obdurate. The IRS had sent its first letter to Bob Jones University in November 1970 to ascertain whether or not it discriminated on the basis of race. The school responded defiantly: It did not admit African Americans.

Although Bob Jones Jr., the school's founder, argued that racial segregation was mandated by the Bible, Falwell and Weyrich quickly sought to shift the grounds of the debate, framing their opposition in terms of religious freedom rather than in defense of racial segregation. For decades, evangelical leaders had boasted that because their educational institutions accepted no federal money (except for, of course, not having to pay taxes), the government could not tell them how to run their shops— whom to hire or not, whom to admit or reject. The *Brown v. Board of Education* decision of 1954 and the Civil Rights Act a decade later, however, changed that calculus.

I remember these arguments from my evangelical childhood. From time to time, the president of a Bible institute or evangelical college would visit my father's congregation, usually for the Sunday evening service. The president would be traveling to raise funds and to recruit students, but one of the boilerplate selling points was always, "We don't accept any federal money; therefore, the government can't tell us what to do." These institutions, like Bob Jones University, had long argued that because they accepted no federal funds, they were immune to government strictures; the federal government could not tell them how to run their institutions.

Such casuistry, however, ignores a crucial fact: Tax exemption is a form of public subsidy. Churches and other nonprofit organizations are required to pay no taxes (other than Social Security tax on wages), which means that taxpaying citizens make up the difference for everything from parks and police protection to national defense.

Weyrich and other founders of the Religious Right cannily sought to shift the justification for their political activism away from a defense of racial segregation and toward a putative defense of religious freedom, all the while ignoring the fact that religious institutions were free to pursue whatever racial policies they chose—so long as they surrendered their tax exemptions. Indeed, the most obvious, commonsense reading of the Religious Right is that conservative evangelicals were mobilizing in defense of racial segregation. Weyrich's sleight of hand brilliantly shifted perceptions of the movement away from racism toward a more high-minded defense of religious freedom. (The Religious Right's later opposition to abortion further burnished its image as a movement crusading against moral evil.)

In the course of the 1970s, Bob Jones University did, in fact, try to placate the IRS—albeit in its own way. Following initial inquiries into the school's racial policies, Bob Jones admitted one African American, a worker in its radio station, WMUU, as a part-time student; he dropped out a month later. In 1975, again in an attempt to forestall IRS action, the school admitted blacks to the student body, but, out of fears of miscegenation, refused to admit *unmarried* African Americans. The school also stipulated that any students who engaged in interracial dating, or who were even associated with organizations that advocated interracial dating, would be expelled.[7]

The IRS was not placated. On January 19, 1976, after years of warnings—integrate or pay taxes—the agency rescinded the school's tax exemption. For many evangelical leaders, who had been following the issue since *Green v. Connally*, Bob Jones University came to be seen as a bellwether. When the IRS declared its intentions in August 1978 to revoke the tax exemptions of schools with an "insignificant number of minority students," Weyrich had his issue: the defense of racially segregated evangelical institutions.[8]

Despite the persistence of the abortion myth—the fiction that the movement began in opposition to *Roe v. Wade*—other early leaders of the Religious Right have corroborated Weyrich's account that the defense of Bob Jones University and other institutions galvanized evangelical leaders into a political force. "The Religious New Right did not start because of a concern about abortion," Ed Dobson, formerly Falwell's assistant at Moral Majority, said in 1990. "I sat in the non-smoke-filled back room with the Moral Majority, and I frankly do not remember abortion being mentioned as a reason why we ought to do something." Another conservative activist, Grover Norquist, confirmed that the *Roe v. Wade* decision did not factor into the rise of the Religious Right. "The religious right did not get started in 1962 with prayer in school," Norquist told Dan Gilgoff, of *U.S. News & World Report*, in June 2009. "And it didn't get started in '73 with *Roe v. Wade*. It started in '77 or '78 with the Carter administration's attack on Christian schools and radio stations. That's where all of the organization flowed out of. It was complete self-defense."[9]

The actions of the Internal Revenue Service especially affected Bob Jones University, goading those associated with the school into political activism. Elmer L. Rumminger, longtime administrator at the university, who became politically active in 1980, remembered that the IRS case "alerted the Christian school community about what could happen with government interference" in the affairs of evangelical institutions. "That was really the major issue that got us all involved to begin with—at least it was for me." What about abortion? "No, no, that wasn't the issue," he said emphatically. "This wasn't an anti-abortion movement per se. That was one of the issues we were interested in. I'm sure some people pointed to *Roe v. Wade*, but that's not what got us going. For me it was government intrusion into private education."[10]

As Bob Jones University sued to retain its tax exemption, Weyrich pressed his case. Evangelical leaders, especially those whose schools were affected by the ruling, were angry, electing to construe the decision as government intrusion in religious matters. Weyrich used the *Green v. Connally* case to rally evangelicals against the government. When "the Internal Revenue Service tried to deny tax exemption to private schools," Weyrich said in an interview with *Conservative Digest*, that "more than any single act brought the fundamentalists and evangelicals into the political process." The IRS action "kicked a sleeping dog," Richard Viguerie, one of the founders of the New Right, said. "It was the episode that ignited the religious right's involvement in real politics." When *Conservative Digest* catalogued evangelical discontent with Jimmy

Carter in August 1979, the Internal Revenue Service regulations headed the list. Abortion, on the other hand, was not mentioned.[11]

In ramping up for political activism, evangelicals portrayed themselves as defending what they considered the sanctity of the evangelical subculture from outside interference. Weyrich astutely picked up on those fears. "What caused the movement to surface was the federal government's moves against Christian schools," Weyrich reiterated in 1990. "This absolutely shattered the Christian community's notions that Christians could isolate themselves inside their own institutions and teach what they pleased." For agitated evangelicals, Weyrich's conservative gospel of less government suddenly struck a responsive chord. "It wasn't the abortion issue; that wasn't sufficient," Weyrich recalled. "It was the recognition that isolation simply would no longer work in this society."[12]

Although leaders of the Religious Right in later years have sought to portray their politicization as a direct response to the *Roe v. Wade* ruling of 1973, Weyrich and other organizers of the Religious Right have emphatically dismissed this abortion myth. *Green v. Connally* served as the catalyst, not *Roe v. Wade*.

More broadly, evangelical leaders, prodded by Weyrich, chose to interpret the IRS ruling against segregationist schools as an assault on the integrity and the sanctity of the evangelical subculture, ignoring the fact that exemption from taxes is itself a form of public subsidy. That is what prompted them to action and to organize into a political movement. Opposition to abortion came later.

What about Abortion?

How did abortion finally become part of the Religious Right's agenda? After mobilizing in opposition to the Internal Revenue Service, Paul Weyrich and leaders of the nascent Religious Right were savvy enough to recognize that they needed another issue besides defense of racial segregation to rally rank-and-file evangelicals to the voting booth. Opposition to abortion, however, was by no means the logical alternative.

Several operatives offered suggestions. Robert Billings, a Bob Jones University alumnus who formed the National Christian Action Coalition to protest IRS actions directed at evangelical schools, thought that opposition to gay rights would energize evangelical voters. "We need an emotionally charged issue to stir up people," he said. "I believe that the homosexual issue is the issue we should use."[1]

In 1977, Anita Bryant, a former Miss Oklahoma and runner-up Miss America, had organized a movement, Save Our Children, to rescind an ordinance in Dade County, Florida, that protected the rights of gays and lesbians. Even Bryant, however, recognized that the school issue and tax exemption lay at the heart of the Religious Right. "I believe the day of the comfortable Christian is over," she declared. "Maybe it hasn't reached everybody in the rural areas, but it's a battle in the cities to keep them from taking over and reaching private and religious schools."[2]

Evangelical voices decrying abortion throughout most of the 1970s were few and far between. On May 17, 1971, the executive committee of Carl McIntire's ultra-fundamentalist organization, the American Council of Christian Churches, had issued a press release affirming "the sanctity of human life" and opposing "abortion on demand." At the opposite end of the political spectrum, following *Roe v. Wade*, Mark O. Hatfield, Republican senator from Oregon and progressive evangelical, cosponsored a proposed constitutional amendment to ban abortion except in cases of rape or when the mother's life was endangered.[3]

Some antiabortion evangelicals contend that the first major statement of evangelical opposition to abortion was "The Passivity of American Christians," written by Harold O. J. Brown and published in the January 16, 1976, issue of *Christianity Today*, three years after the *Roe v. Wade* decision. The article does indeed say that "the overwhelming testimony of Christians from the earliest days to the present has been one of opposition to abortion except in cases involving a serious threat to the life of the mother," but this appears as one example among several in the author's larger argument calling on evangelicals to let their voices be heard on cultural issues.[4]

Not long thereafter, Weyrich approached William Brock, former senator from Tennessee and head of the Republican National Committee, to ask for help mobilizing evangelical voters in advance of the midterm elections of 1978. His appeal fell on deaf ears; the chair of the committee "didn't understand what I was talking about," Weyrich recounted. "It was so foreign to him that it didn't make any sense." Undeterred, Weyrich resolved to "go out and elect some improbable people in the '78 elections."[5]

The midterm elections in 1978, when pro-life

Republicans defeated favored Democratic candidates in New Hampshire, Iowa, and Minnesota, persuaded Weyrich that opposition to abortion could work as a populist issue. In those races, antiabortion activists (principally Roman Catholics) leafleted church parking lots on the final weekend of the campaign; two days later, in a plebiscite with a very low turnout, the favored Democratic candidates lost.

In Iowa, for example, polls and pundits expected that the incumbent Democratic senator, Richard C. "Dick" Clark, would coast easily to reelection; no poll heading into the November balloting indicated that Clark held a lead of fewer than ten percentage points. Six years earlier, Clark had walked across the state to call attention to his grassroots, upstart challenge to Jack Miller, the two-term Republican incumbent, and Clark prevailed with 55 percent of the vote. He remained a popular figure in the state. Antiabortion activists, however, had targeted Clark, and on the final weekend of Clark's reelection campaign, representatives of Iowans for Life (predominantly Roman Catholics) distributed approximately 300,000 pamphlets in church parking lots. Two days later, in a low-turnout election, Roger Jepsen, the Republican pro-life challenger, defeated Clark.

An election day survey by the *Des Moines Register* indicated that about twenty-five thousand Iowans voted for Jepsen because of his stand on abortion. "I personally believe that the abortion issue was the central issue," Clark told Bruce Morton of CBS News. The senator's campaign manager agreed. "It comes right down to those leaflets they put out," he said.[6]

Christianity Today noted Clark's unexpected defeat, and the magazine also credited pro-lifers for the Republican trifecta in Minnesota, where Republican candidates who opposed abortion captured both Senate seats (one for the unexpired term of Hubert Humphrey) and the office of governor. "Anti-abortionists figured in the collapse of Minnesota's liberal Democratic-Farmer-Labor Party," the magazine reported, adding that the campaign of Albert Quie, the governor-elect and ally of Charles Colson, "distributed 250,000 leaflets to churchgoers throughout the state on the Sunday before election day."[7]

In the course of my research in Falwell's archives at Liberty University and Weyrich's papers at the University of Wyoming, it became very clear that the 1978 election represented a formative step toward galvanizing everyday evangelical voters. Correspondence between Weyrich and evangelical leaders fairly crackles with excitement. In a letter to fellow conservative Daniel B. Hales, Weyrich characterized the triumph of pro-life candidates as "true cause for celebration." Billings, a cobelligerent who had urged opposition to gay rights as the "emotionally charged issue to stir up" evangelical voters, now predicted that opposition to abortion would "pull together many of our 'fringe' Christian friends." By this time, *Roe v. Wade* had been law for more than five years.[8]

Weyrich, Falwell, and leaders of the emerging Religious Right enlisted an unlikely ally in their quest to advance abortion as a political issue among evangelicals: Francis A. Schaeffer, a goateed, knickers-wearing theologian who was warning about the eclipse of Christian values and the advance of something he called "secular humanism." Schaeffer, considered by many the intellectual godfather of the Religious Right, was not known for his political activism, but by the late 1970s, he warned that legalized abortion would lead inevitably to infanticide and euthanasia, and he was eager to sound the alarm. Schaeffer teamed with a pediatric surgeon from Philadelphia, C. Everett Koop, on a series of films entitled *Whatever Happened to the Human Race?* In the early months of 1979, Schaeffer and Koop, targeting an evangelical audience, toured the country with these films, which depicted the scourge of abortion in graphic terms—most memorably with a scene of plastic baby dolls strewn along the shores of the Dead Sea. Schaeffer and Koop argued that any society that countenanced abortion was captive to "secular humanism" and therefore caught in a vortex of moral decay.

Between Weyrich's machinations and Schaeffer's jeremiad, evangelicals were slowly coming around on the abortion issue. Protestants, especially evangelicals, according to Schaeffer, "have been so sluggish on this issue of human life, and *Whatever Happened to the Human Race?* is causing real waves, among church people and governmental people too." At the conclusion of the film tour in March 1979, Frank Schaeffer, Francis Schaeffer's son and director of the series, reported: "We were calling for civil disobedience, the takeover of the Republican Party, and even hinting at overthrowing our 'unjust pro-abortion government.'" Even so, Frank Schaeffer insists that the audiences were far smaller than for Schaeffer's previous series, released in 1976, *How Should We Then Live?*[9]

By 1980, even though Jimmy Carter had sought, both as governor of Georgia and as president, to reduce the incidence of abortion, his refusal to seek a constitutional amendment outlawing it was viewed by politically conservative evangelicals as an unpardonable sin. Never mind the fact that his Republican opponent that year, Ronald Reagan, had signed into law, as governor of California in 1967, the most liberal abortion bill in the country.[10]

.

PART THREE

So What?

8

The 1980 Presidential Election

Although *Newsweek* had christened 1976 "The Year of the Evangelical," that declaration may have been four years premature. As the 1980 presidential election approached, not one or two but three candidates contended for the White House as evangelical Christians. Jimmy Carter, the Democratic incumbent, had established his credentials as a "born-again" Christian during his run for the presidency four years earlier. John B. Anderson, Republican member of Congress from Illinois, competed for the Republican nomination and then mounted a third-party bid; Anderson was a longtime member of First Evangelical Free Church in Rockford, Illinois. On the face of it, Ronald Reagan, a divorced and remarried former actor in Hollywood, a province not known to evangelicals for its piety, may have had the weakest claim on evangelical credentials. But when James Robison, a televangelist from Dallas, Texas, asked Reagan about his faith, Reagan told the preacher that Jesus was more real to him than his own mother.[1]

On August 22, 1980, Reagan, the Republican nominee for president, strode to the podium before a packed crowd of fifteen thousand to twenty thousand evangelicals (estimates vary) at Reunion Arena in Dallas. Having been coached beforehand, Reagan flawlessly delivered his line. "Now, I know this is a non-partisan gathering, and so I know that you can't endorse me," he said, pausing for dramatic effect, "but I only brought that up because I want you to know that I endorse you and what you are doing." The line brought down the house and arguably sealed the evangelical vote for Reagan.[2]

The candidate went on to declare his support for creationism and said that if he were stranded on a desert island, the one book he would want with him was the Bible. Reflecting the fury of evangelical leaders with the attempts to rescind the tax exemption of racially segregated institutions, Reagan excoriated the "unconstitutional regulatory agenda" directed by the Internal Revenue Service "against independent schools." His speech before a packed house of evangelicals made no mention whatsoever of abortion.[3]

Publicly, Paul Weyrich was ecstatic. "We gave him a ten-minute standing ovation," he recalled later. "I've never seen anything like it. The whole movement was snowballing by then." Privately, however, Weyrich, who had worked so assiduously to change the topic from a defense of racial segregation, confided to conservative allies that he was not pleased with Reagan's remarks. He noted that the candidate nearly canceled his appearance because, Weyrich said, "aides feared a backlash if Reagan were too closely identified with the so-called Christian Right." Writing three days after the event, Weyrich complained: "Reagan aides constructed a speech for the candidate which had just enough emotional appeal for the audience, but which carefully avoided the issues of abortion, the Equal Rights Amendment, Gay Rights and Prayer in the Schools, each of which is a bottom line issue with the Evangelical/Fundamentalist community represented at the gathering."[4]

Carter lost the 1980 election for a variety of reasons, not merely the opposition of the Religious Right. He faced a spirited challenge from within his own party; Edward M. Kennedy's failed quest for the Democratic nomination undermined Carter's support among liberals. And because election day fell on the anniversary of the taking of American hostages in Iran, the media played up the story, highlighting Carter's inability to secure the hostages' freedom. The electorate, once enamored of Carter's evangelical probity, had tired of a sour economy, chronic energy shortages, and the Soviet Union's renewed imperial ambitions.

After the election results came in, Jerry Falwell, never shy about claiming credit, was fond of quoting a Harris poll that suggested Carter would have won the popular vote by a margin of 1 percent had it not been for the machinations of the Religious Right. "I knew that we would have some impact on the national elections," Falwell said, "but I had no idea that it would be this great."[5]

Given Carter's political troubles, the defection of evangelicals may or may not have been decisive. But it is certainly true that evangelicals, having helped propel Carter to the White House four years earlier, turned dramatically against him, their fellow evangelical, during the course of his presidency. And the catalyst for their political activism was not, as often claimed, opposition to abortion. Although abortion had begun to emerge as a rallying cry late in the 1980 campaign, the real roots of the Religious Right lay not in the defense of a fetus but in the defense of racial segregation.

Why the Abortion Myth Matters

Following the election of Ronald Reagan in November 1980, the Religious Right was eager to consolidate its gains. The 1980 Republican Party platform had included a pledge to "halt the unconstitutional regulatory vendetta launched by Mr. Carter's IRS commissioner against independent schools," and the Religious Right sought to shield evangelical institutions from the Internal Revenue Service. Reagan appointed Robert Billings, one of the founders of Moral Majority, as director of regional offices in the Department of Education. Billings used his post to fend off the IRS in its attempts to rescind the tax exemption of racially segregated schools.[1]

On the abortion front, evangelical leaders pressed the president-elect to appoint C. Everett Koop, copresenter of *Whatever Happened to the Human Race?*, as surgeon general. Reagan agreed. By the conclusion of Reagan's first term, many grass-roots evangelicals had fully embraced the antiabortion movement. Some openly declared themselves single-issue voters.

So, what does it matter that their political movement, the Religious Right, grew out of (to put it plainly) racism, a defense of racial segregation in evangelical institutions? On the face of it, it matters not at all. I have no reason to doubt the sincerity of evangelicals who oppose abortion—some have devoted their entire lives to this cause—even as I suspect the motives of those who brought the issue to their attention.

I believe the abortion myth matters because unacknowledged and unaddressed racism has a tendency to fester. Black codes and Jim Crow laws emerged out of the "magnolia myth," the enduring fiction that blacks were inferior. Jon Meacham has pointed out that the 1866 publication *The Lost Cause: A New Southern History of the War of the Confederates* created a mythology of the virtuous, slaveholding South and enshrined the notion of white supremacy as "the true cause of the war" and the "true hope of the South." Ghettos sprang up in Northern cities because of lack of opportunities in the workplace;

misguided, racially skewed government policies; the intentional construction of lily-white communities; and the practice of redlining, the refusal to sell real estate to African Americans or to write mortgages in selected neighborhoods. Police brutality against people of color persists because of stereotyping and lack of attention to racial profiling.[2]

I have often defended evangelicals against the charge of racism, but the results of the 2016 presidential election, when 81 percent of white evangelicals voted for Donald Trump, forced me to reconsider and to see the history of the Religious Right in a new light. Whereas I had once believed that a commitment to "family values" and opposition to abortion had indeed replaced racism at the core of the movement, I now suspect otherwise.

Let's go back to the 1980 presidential campaign, when evangelicals rejected one of their own, a Sunday school teacher and "born-again" Christian—the white Southerner who had dispatched George Wallace and turned his party finally and squarely against racism—in favor of the divorced and re-married former governor of California. Reagan was the first political figure embraced by the Religious Right, whose leaders have elevated him to something akin to patron saint. Is there something about Ronald Reagan that prefigured the racism of the Religious Right?[3]

Reagan, an FBI informer during the McCarthy era, plunged into California politics in 1964 to support the repeal of the Rumford Fair Housing Act, which sought to eliminate racial discrimination in the rental and sale of residential properties. On the federal level, Reagan opposed both the Civil Rights Act of 1964 and the Voting Rights Act of 1965, positions that prefigured his opposition to affirmative action, which he characterized as "reverse discrimination." By the time Reagan geared up his campaign for governor in 1966, the *Los Angeles Sentinel*, an African American newspaper, wrote that, despite the candidate's protestations that he was not a racist, "Mr. Reagan is rapidly assuming the stature as the outstanding American spokesman for racism." The paper continued: "Judged by his actions alone, and discounting his words of self-praise, Mr. Reagan cannot be distinguished from Governor George Wallace of Alabama."[4]

Reagan's 1966 gubernatorial campaign (and others thereafter) made liberal use of the slogan "law and order," a phrase with racist undertones that, like "states' rights," is generally construed as code language for keeping blacks in their place. As Robert L. Coate of the California Democratic Party observed, "Reagan handles racism in such a manner that racists understand exactly what he is saying, without his having to spell it out for them." In a 1971 conversation taped by Richard Nixon, Reagan remarked about "those monkeys from those African countries—damn them, they're still uncomfortable wearing shoes!"[5]

Racist tropes carried over into Reagan's 1980 campaign for president. In January of that year, Reagan addressed a cheering crowd of more than six thousand at Bob Jones University. He excoriated the IRS, pronounced the school a "great institution," and was interrupted by applause fourteen times, three of them standing ovations.[6]

On August 3, 1980, with the Republican nomination in hand, Reagan opened his general election campaign for the presidency in, of all places, Philadelphia, Mississippi, the community where sixteen years earlier, members of the Ku Klux Klan, with the collusion of the sheriff's office, abducted, beat, and murdered three civil rights workers. Reagan, the master of symbolism, might have used the macabre setting to put to rest any lingering suspicions that his campaign would appeal to racism in any form. Instead, in front of twenty thousand whites, many of them waving Confederate flags and chanting "We want Reagan!," the candidate invoked the defiant battle cry of George C. Wallace and countless other segregationists: "I believe in states' rights."[7]

Reagan, who openly supported the apartheid states of Rhodesia and South Africa, employed other racist dog whistles in the course of the campaign, including his vile caricature of "welfare queens," mythical people of color who allegedly wallow in riches by bilking public assistance programs. My purpose here is not to judge whether or not Reagan himself was a racist; I'll let his words and actions speak for themselves. The point is that someone, either Reagan himself or someone directing the Reagan-Bush campaign, calculated that racially coded language and gestures would appeal to voters—including, perhaps, newly enfranchised Religious Right voters.

As president, Reagan proceeded systematically to emasculate the Civil Rights Commission, the independent, bipartisan watchdog created by the Civil Rights Act of 1957. The venerable Theodore Hesburgh, president of the University of Notre Dame and a charter member of the commission, described it as the nation's "conscience in the matter of civil rights." Using maneuvers of dubious legality, however, Reagan dismissed commission members and replaced them with appointees who took a dim view of women's rights and civil rights, one of whom had called for the abolition of the Civil Rights Commission itself. The Reagan administration's machinations prompted Parren J. Mitchell, longtime African American member of Congress from Maryland, to accuse Reagan of "attempting the political rape" of the commission.[8]

Aside from Reagan, the Religious Right's avatar, I think it's also fair to look at the leaders of the Religious Right themselves. Although he later repented of it, Jerry Falwell denounced the landmark *Brown v. Board of Education* ruling, which mandated the desegregation of public schools. "If Chief Justice Warren and his associates had known God's word and had desired to do the Lord's will, I am quite confident that the 1954 decision would never have been made," Falwell preached. "The facilities should be separate. When God has drawn a line of distinction, we should not attempt to cross that line." Integra-

tion, Falwell warned, "will destroy our race eventually." Falwell referred to the Civil Rights Act of
1964 as "civil wrongs," and in 1967, the same year
the Commonwealth of Virginia finally mandated
the desegregation of the state's public schools, Falwell formed his own segregated school, Lynchburg
Christian Academy, which the *Lynchburg News* described as "a private school for white students."
When asked by a local minister if blacks would be
admitted, Falwell said no.[9]

Falwell's most famous sermon, "Of Ministers
and Marches," was delivered on a Sunday evening,
March 21, 1965, from the pulpit of Thomas Road
Baptist Church. Two weeks earlier, on what became known as Bloody Sunday, civil rights protesters were met by Alabama state troopers after they
crossed the Edmund Pettus Bridge on their march
from Selma to Montgomery to protest racism and
the police brutality that led to the death of Jimmie
Lee Jackson in nearby Marion. With the protection
of a court order, the march to Montgomery resumed
two Sundays later, prompting Falwell that evening
to denounce Martin Luther King Jr. as a communist
subversive and to insist that, "Believing the Bible as
I do, I would find it impossible to stop preaching the

pure saving gospel of Jesus Christ, and begin doing anything else—including fighting communism, or participating in civil rights reforms."[10]

Other early leaders of the Religious Right shared similar suspicions of black leaders and civil rights. Tim LaHaye, for example, a graduate of Bob Jones University and, later, one of the charter board members for Moral Majority, wrote a letter upbraiding the president of Wheaton College for allowing an event on campus honoring the memory of King shortly after his assassination. LaHaye characterized the civil rights leader as "an out-right theological liberal heretic."[11]

Weyrich himself acknowledged the absence of African Americans and people of color in the Religious Right. "I'm not going to kid you that we have minorities running out our ears," he told the *New York Times* in 1980. "This is not a minority movement."[12]

With several notable exceptions, leaders of the Religious Right have learned to modulate their language and their comportment in the decades since the emergence of the movement. Several, like Falwell himself, have apologized for their racist views and statements.

Not everyone, however. While running the senatorial campaign of his political mentor, Woody Jenkins, in 1996, Tony Perkins, a graduate of Falwell's Liberty University, paid $82,500 to purchase direct-call services from a company owned by David Duke, grand imperial wizard of the Ku Klux Klan. On May 17, 2001, while running for the Senate himself, Perkins addressed the Louisiana chapter of the white supremacist Council of Conservative Citizens, the successor of the White Citizens' Council, also known informally as the "uptown Klan." The Council of Conservative Citizens describes African Americans as "a retrograde species of humanity," and in 2001, the same year Perkins addressed the gathering, the organization's website asserted that "God is the author of racism" and "Mixing the races is rebelliousness against God." I've found no record of Perkins's remarks on May 17, 2001, but a local newspaper ran a photograph showing Perkins, then a state representative, standing at the lectern in Bonanno's Restaurant in Baton Rouge, the state capital, a big smile on his face and a Confederate flag hanging directly behind him. According to the photo caption, Perkins was surrounded by officers of the Louisiana chapter of the Council of Conservative Citizens. Perkins finished fourth in Louisiana's 2002 Republican primary; the following year, he was appointed head of James Dobson's Family Research Council, a prominent Religious Right organization.[13]

After he was removed from the Alabama Supreme Court for disobeying a court order, Roy S. Moore, the notorious "Ten Commandments Judge," formed his own Religious Right organization, the Foundation for Moral Law. In both 2009 and 2010, Moore's group sponsored pro-Confederate Alabama "Secession Day" events. Moore, who claims to be a Baptist, has called for eliminating the Fourteenth Amendment to the Constitution, the amendment that guaranteed former slaves equal protection under the law. In 2017, Moore mounted his own campaign for the Senate as the Republican nominee in a special election. During a campaign event, an African American man asked the candidate when America was last great. Moore replied, "I think it was great at the time when families were united—even though we had slavery—they cared for one another."[14]

No one has mastered racially coded language better than Donald Trump, who harvested the overwhelming majority of white evangelical votes in 2016 and 2020. Trump, also the master of publicity, clawed his way to public attention by perpetrating the so-called birther conspiracy, the malevolent falsehood that Barack Obama was born in Kenya, not the United States, and was therefore constitutionally ineligible to be president.

An exhaustive listing of Trump's racist statements and actions—from his branding of Mexican immigrants as "rapists" and "criminals" and his defense of white supremacists to his treatment of refugees from Latin America—need not be recounted here. "Trump ran openly on racial grievance," Stuart Stevens, a Republican consultant, said. "It was hatred and fear of Muslims, Hispanics and Blacks." Stevens characterized 2016 as the "most openly racial campaign by a president since Andrew Johnson." The real question is, why did 81 percent of white evangelicals vote for Trump in 2016 and 78 percent in 2020? And why do evangelical leaders refuse to condemn his racism?[15]

For decades, leaders of the Religious Right have assured us that theirs was a movement devoted to "family values," a statement that is difficult to reconcile with support for a thrice-married former casino operator and self-confessed sexual predator who cavorts with a porn star. Could it be—could it be?—that the 2016 election finally allowed the Religious Right to abandon the pretext that the embrace of family values lay at the core of their movement, that support for Donald Trump represents the movement coming full circle to the charter principle behind its formation?

There is a kind of tragic continuity in the Religious Right's embrace of Donald Trump. A movement that began with the defense of racial segregation in the late 1970s climbed into bed with a vulgar demagogue who recognizes "some good people" among white supremacists, who equivocates about denouncing a representative of the Ku Klux Klan, and who admonished a white supremacist terrorist group to "stand by" in advance of the 2020 election. If racism is America's original sin, politically conservative evangelicals, with their continuing support for their champion, have been loath to seek redemption.

Sadly, the Religious Right was never about the advancement of biblical values. The modern, politically conservative evangelical activism we see today is a movement rooted in the perpetuation of racial segregation, and its affiliation with the hard-right fringes of the conservative movement beginning in the late 1970s produced a mutant form of evangelicalism inconsistent with the best traditions of evangelicalism itself.[16]

Rather than reclaim the reforming zeal of their forebears, who sought to make the world a better place by caring for those on the margins, politically conservative evangelicals cast their lot with someone who stands squarely outside of the evangelical tradition, someone either unfamiliar with or contemptuous of the long and noble tradition of evangelical social reform. The latter part of that description applies as well to the leaders of the Religious Right. If they are unfamiliar with their own tradition, they have passed on the opportunity to be guided by the example of worthy predecessors; more likely, given the politicians and the policies they support, leaders of the Religious Right hold that tradition in contempt. Whatever the case, having thereby forfeited their prophetic voice, leaders of the movement and the Religious Right itself have become little more than a political interest group.

This is not to say that all evangelicals are racists. Not at all. The leaders of the Religious Right have been so successful in obfuscating the origins of their movement that most evangelical voters, I'm confident, are unaware that the catalyst for their political activism was a defense of racial segregation. I don't even discount the possibility that, despite overwhelming and conclusive evidence to the contrary, some of the organizers themselves have come to believe the abortion myth. In an interview shortly before his death, Jerry Falwell offered his own revisionist history: "We were simply driven into the process by *Roe v. Wade* and earlier than that, the expulsion of God from the public square." The beauty of the abortion myth is that it conceals an uglier truth.[17]

And that is precisely the point. Leaders of the Religious Right can gussy up their movement by rallying behind such high-minded issues as opposition to abortion or (disingenuously) religious freedom, but that does not change the inconvenient fact that the founders of the movement in the 1970s organized to allow evangelical institutions to perpetuate their policies of racial exclusion. A building can feature all sorts of dazzling baubles and filigree, but if the timbers that make up its foundation are rotten, the entire structure is compromised.

Tragically, the 2016 and 2020 elections suggest to me that racism may have some lingering appeal for some percentage of white evangelical voters—or, at the very least, it does not repel them. And I wonder, in turn, if that can be attributed to a failure to address the racism that lies at the core of the Religious Right. Unacknowledged and unaddressed racism has a tendency to fester. In the words of Scripture and in words invoked by Abraham Lincoln, "A house divided against itself shall not stand."[18]

The specter of racism surfaces at times in unexpected ways. In February 2019, a group of self-described "pro-family leaders," including James Dobson, sent a letter to the Republican leadership in the House of Representatives in defense of Steve King, representative from Iowa with a long history of racist and white supremacist rhetoric, including a declaration that "We can't restore our civilization with somebody else's babies." In an interview with the *New York Times*, King asked, "White nationalist, white supremacist, Western civilization—how did that language become offensive?" The letter from Religious Right leaders called King, who routinely disparaged immigrants and minorities, "an outstanding member of Congress" who has "served honorably and faithfully for 16 years." King's colleague and Religious Right favorite, Louie Gohmert of Texas, defended King in a speech from the House floor.[19]

Racism, or at least a tolerance for racism, also

surfaces in evangelical refusals to denounce Trump's racist demagoguery. When Trump asked why the United States should accept refugees from "shithole countries," Robert Jeffress, pastor of First Baptist Church in Dallas, Texas, replied, "Apart from the vocabulary attributed to him, President Trump is right on target in his sentiment." Jerry Falwell Jr., son of the founder of Moral Majority, said of Trump that "evangelicals have found their dream president." Ralph Reed, head of the Faith & Freedom Coalition, declared that "it should be clear to all evangelical Christians that President Trump is the leader we need." Franklin Graham, who promoted Trump's false "birther" allegations, said he believed that God put Trump in office and described him as "the most pro-life-friendly president in American history."[20]

Part of the collateral damage of the abortion myth and the concomitant alliance of evangelicalism with the hard-right elements of the Republican Party is that the debate over abortion itself has become stale and ossified. What should be a lively moral conversation devolved long ago into dualistic and partisan sloganeering. As Daniel K. Williams has demonstrated, the "pro-life" movement before *Roe v. Wade* was diverse and included New

Deal liberals as well as civil rights and human rights activists. The cause was once embraced by such prominent progressives as Edward M. Kennedy, Joseph R. Biden Jr., Jesse Jackson, and (as we have seen) Mark O. Hatfield. The Republican Party, on the other hand, included "pro-choice" politicians throughout the 1970s, including George H. W. Bush, who famously switched his allegiance only after Reagan, himself a recent convert to the antiabortion cause, tapped him as running mate in 1980.[21]

I have heard from several pioneer opponents of abortion who speak nostalgically about the early years of the movement. It was a time of great excitement and energy, they say, with diverse voices offering judicious, nuanced arguments against abortion. What happened? Conservatives, led in part by Paul Weyrich, commandeered the antiabortion movement, calling for legislation outlawing abortion (somewhat improbably for an ideology that professes to champion individual liberties and small government).

As the antiabortion movement became associated with right-wing politics, at the same time that the Democratic Party began to emphasize women's rights and reproductive freedom, the issue—pro-choice *ver-*

sus pro-life—began to divide along party lines to the point that a pro-life Democrat became an endangered species and most Republican politicians recognized that their hopes of securing their party's nomination for almost any office was imperiled if they took a nuanced position on abortion.

The logical, unfortunate, even tragic corollary to this partisan dualism is single-issue voting. Rather than evaluate overall policies and platforms, too many citizens (on both sides of the issue) decided to cast their votes solely on the basis of abortion. A candidate or a party could have ruinous economic proposals or execrable policies on race or poverty or the environment, but as long as they lined up on the "right" side of the abortion issue, they would be assured of support. In the case of the 2016 election, a candidate might be ethically compromised, a racist, and show no signs of a moral compass, but once he delivered the appropriate rhetoric about abortion, he secured the allegiance of the Religious Right, even if that rhetoric contradicted his earlier positions.

Single-issue voting on abortion makes white evangelicals complicit on a whole range of policies that would be anathema to nineteenth-century evangelical reformers, not to mention the Bible itself. How is a ruthless exclusionary policy toward immigrants and refugees in any way consistent with scriptural mandates to welcome the stranger and treat the foreigner as one of your own? How does environmental destruction and indifference to climate change honor God's creation? One of evangelicals' signature issues in the nineteenth century was support for "common schools" because they provided a boost for the children of those less fortunate; Trump's secretary of education (who professes to be an evangelical) spent her adult life seeking systematically to undermine, if not destroy, public education. Evangelical positions on poverty, racial justice, women's equality, or access to health care should surely be calibrated with Jesus's injunctions to care for widows and orphans, to feed the hungry and clothe the naked, and with Paul's declaration that in Christ there is no distinction between Jew and gentile, slave and free, male and female.

I'm not asking white evangelicals to abandon their opposition to abortion (even though I believe many of those efforts are misdirected). But abortion should be considered in a larger context, and the path to healing lies in facing the past and dealing with it forthrightly. Repentance, in my experience, is good for the soul.

Once evangelicals come to terms with the abortion myth and the racism baked into the Religious Right, I dare to hope that they might then reexamine other aspects of their political agenda, an agenda that has been inordinately dictated by the fusion of the Religious Right with the far-right precincts of the Republican Party. A fresh reading of Jesus's injunctions to feed the hungry and welcome the stranger or an appreciation for evangelical social reform in the nineteenth century might prompt evangelicals to reconsider their views on immigration and public education, their attitudes about prison reform and women's rights, or their support of tax cuts for the affluent. Jesus, after all, enjoined his followers to care for "the least of these," and taking those words seriously could very well prompt a redirection of evangelical political energies, even a rethinking of single-issue voting in favor of a broader, more comprehensive appraisal of political agendas. Such a reconsideration might also provide an opening for rapprochement with black evangelicals and other evangelicals of color.

Repentance is good for the soul.

Postscript

Two developments related to this narrative merit mention.

First, Bob Jones University lost its tax-exempt status, after years of warnings, on January 19, 1976. When Jimmy Carter was running for reelection in 1980, one of the Religious Right's complaints against him was that his Internal Revenue Service was stripping evangelical institutions of their tax exemptions.

A second look at that date, January 19, 1976, reveals how scurrilous that charge was. January 19, 1976, was an important date for Carter, but not because he was in any way responsible for the action against Bob Jones University. That was the day he won a plurality in the Iowa precinct caucuses, his first major step toward winning the Democratic nomination for president. Carter assumed office a year and a day *after* Bob Jones University lost its tax exemption. Gerald R. Ford was president when that happened, not Carter.

The second development is related. In January 1982, the Reagan administration announced that it was rescinding the IRS directive that denied tax exemptions to racially discriminatory private schools, thereby restoring Bob Jones University's tax-exempt status. A public outcry forced the administration to reconsider; Ronald Reagan backpedaled by saying that the legislature should determine such matters, not the judiciary. Bob Jones University's appeal finally reached the US Supreme Court in October of the same year, with the university arguing that it should be allowed to retain both its tax exemption and its racial policies. Because the Reagan administration had effectively abandoned the case, the court took the unusual step of appointing a third party—William T. Coleman, a cabinet member in the Ford administration and chair of the NAACP Legal Defense Fund—to submit a brief in defense of the IRS position.[1]

The Supreme Court's decision in the *Bob Jones University v. United States* case, handed down on May 24, 1983, ruled against the university in an 8–1 decision. Three years later, Reagan elevated the sole dissenter, William Rehnquist, to chief justice of the Supreme Court.[2]

Notes

PREFACE

1. Michael Cromartie, ed., *No Longer Exiles: The Religious New Right in American Politics* (Washington, DC: Ethics and Public Policy Center, 1993), 52. This volume is the published proceedings of that conference.

2. I'm grateful to Norman Bendroth, a contemporary at Trinity Evangelical Divinity School who later worked for Brown's organization, Christian Action Council, for confirming my recollections about Brown and the abortion issue at the school; telephone conversation, August 18, 2020. In the interest of full disclosure, I should probably reveal that I wrote my MA thesis, under the direction of John D. Woodbridge, on the topic of biblical inerrancy; see Randall Balmer, "The Princetonians and Scripture: A Reconsideration," *Westminster Theological Journal* 44 (1982): 352–65; Balmer, "The Princetonians, Scripture, and Recent Scholarship," *Journal of Presbyterian History* 60 (1982): 267–70.

DEFINITIONS AND TERMS

1. I generally avoid the terms "fundamentalist" and "fundamentalism" in this book—not because they aren't useful, but because they are so frequently misused. The term "fundamentalism" derives from a series of pamphlets published between 1910 and 1915 by theologically conservative Protestants in an effort to stanch the drift toward liberalism in Protestant denominations. Those who subscribed to the doctrines set forth in these pamphlets (including the virgin birth of Jesus, the authenticity of miracles, and the inerrancy of the Scriptures) came to be known as fundamentalists. The word has since been applied to other religious traditions—Hindu fundamentalists, Jewish fundamentalists, Mormon fundamentalists, Muslim fundamentalists, et al.—but the term belongs properly to American religious history. "Fundamentalism" has come to denote a kind of militancy in addition to (in the American context) separatism and sectarianism. It applies to the Religious Right in that it tends to be relentlessly dualistic in its view of the world.

2. In his sketch of the historical background of the Religious Right, George Marsden cites as one of the precedents what he calls a "Conscience Coalition," beginning in the antebellum period and extending into the twentieth century, but the politics of this movement, as he points out, would not generally be aligned on the right

of the political spectrum. See George Marsden, "The Religious Right: A Historical Overview," in *No Longer Exiles: The Religious New Right in American Politics*, ed. Michael Cromartie (Washington, DC: Ethics and Public Policy Center, 1993), chap. 1.

CHAPTER ONE

1. Silliman, quoted in George P. Fisher, *Life of Benjamin Silliman, M.D., LL.D.*, 2 vols. (New York: Charles Scribner, 1866), 1:83; Samuel Merwin and Nathaniel William Taylor," Revival in New-Haven," *Christian Spectator* 3 (January 1821): 49-52; "Revival of Religion in Yale College," *Connecticut Evangelical Magazine and Religious Intelligencer* 8 (May 1815): 192; "Revival in Yale College," *Mutual Rights and Methodist Protestant*, May 20, 1831, 157. See also "Yale College," *Religious Intelligencer,* April 7, 1821, 736. On the Second Awakening in New England, see David W. Kling, *A Field of Divine Wonders: The New Divinity and Village Revivals in Northwestern Connecticut, 1792-1822* (State College: Pennsylvania State University Press, 1993). See also John R. Fitzmier, *New England's Moral Legislator: Timothy Dwight, 1752-1817* (Indianapolis and Bloomington: Indiana University Press, 1998).

2. On the Great Revival, see John B. Boles, *The Great Revival: Beginnings of the Bible Belt* (Lexington: University Press of Kentucky, 1996); Christine Leigh Heyrman,

Southern Cross: The Beginnings of the Bible Belt (Chapel Hill: University of North Carolina Press, 1998).

3. "Revival in Rochester, N.Y.," *Christian Advocate & Journal*, April 28, 1827, 134; "Revival at Rochester," *Baptist Chronicle*, December 1, 1830, 190; "Religious Revivals," *Rhode Island Journal*, May 27, 1831, 42; "Revival at Rochester, N.Y." *Morning Star*, June 13, 1833, 27; "Revivals among the Africans in Rochester," *African Repository & Colonial Journal*, April 1, 1831, 61.

4. Charles G. Finney, *Sermons on Gospel Themes* (Oberlin, OH: E. J. Goodrich, 1876), 348, 356.

5. "Thoughts on the Importance and Improvement of Common Schools," *Christian Spectator*, n.s., 1 (February 1827): 85.

CHAPTER TWO

1. There are many sources on dispensationalism. See, for example, Ernest R. Sandeen, *The Roots of Fundamentalism: British and American Millenarianism, 1800-1930* (Chicago: University of Chicago Press, 1970); Donald H. Akenson, *Exporting the Rapture: John Nelson Darby and the Victorian Conquest of North-American Evangelicalism* (New York: Oxford University Press, 2018). Akenson insists that his book is not a biography of Darby; it also focuses much more on Britain than on the United States.

2. For a biographical sketch of Donald Thompson

and the popularity of *A Thief in the Night*, see Randall Balmer, *Mine Eyes Have Seen the Glory: A Journey into the Evangelical Subculture in America*, 5th ed. (New York: Oxford University Press, 2014), chap. 3.

CHAPTER THREE

1. The best account of the trial is Edward J. Larson, *Summer for the Gods: The Scopes Trial and America's Continuing Debate over Science and Religion* (New York: Basic Books, 2006).

2. Mencken, quoted in Michael Shermer, *Why Darwin Matters: The Case against Intelligent Design* (New York: Holt, 2006), 26; Mencken, quoted in Lou Marinoff, *The Middle Way: Finding Happiness in a World of Extremes* (New York: Sterling, 2007), 215.

3. On the construction of evangelical institutions in these decades, see Joel A. Carpenter, *Revive Us Again: The Reawakening of American Fundamentalism* (New York: Oxford University Press, 1999).

CHAPTER FOUR

1. On the so-called evangelical Left, see David R. Swartz, *Moral Minority: The Evangelical Left in an Age of Conservatism* (Philadelphia: University of Pennsylvania Press, 2012).

2. Udall, quoted in Marshall Frady, *Southerners: A Journalistic Odyssey* (New York: New American Library, 1980), 354, 344.

3. Quoted in Daniel K. Williams, *God's Own Party: The Making of the Christian Right* (New York: Oxford University Press, 2012), 126.

CHAPTER FIVE

1. Jerry Falwell, *Strength for the Journey* (New York: Simon & Schuster, 1987), 334–35.

2. Walter O. Spitzer and Carlyle L. Saylor, eds., *Birth Control and the Christian: A Protestant Symposium on the Control of Human Reproduction* (Wheaton, IL: Tyndale House, 1969), 414, xxv–xxviii.

3. Mark Tooley, *Methodism and Politics in the Twentieth Century* (Anderson, IN: Bristol House, 2012), 222, 224–25.

4. *Annual of the Southern Baptist Convention, 1972* (Nashville: Executive Committee, Southern Baptist Convention, 1972), 72. On the reaffirmations of the 1971 resolution, see *Annual of the Southern Baptist Convention, 1974* (Nashville: Executive Committee, Southern Baptist Convention, 1974), 76. The 1976 resolution was more measured, calling on "Southern Baptists and all citizens of the nation to work to change those attitudes and conditions which encourage many people to turn to

abortion as a means of birth control"; but it also affirmed "our conviction about the limited role of government in dealing with matters relating to abortion, and support the right of expectant mothers to the full range of medical services and personal counseling for the preservation of life and health." *Annual of the Southern Baptist Convention, 1976* (Nashville: Executive Committee, Southern Baptist Convention, 1976), 58.

5. Criswell, quoted in "What Price Abortion?" *Christianity Today*, March 2, 1973, 39.

6. Garrett, quoted in "What Price Abortion?" *Christianity Today*, March 2, 1973, 39; Floyd Robertson, in *United Evangelical Action*, Summer 1973, 8–11 (quotes from 11).

7. "Abortion and the Court," *Christianity Today*, February 16, 1973, 32; "Is Abortion a Catholic Issue," *Christianity Today*, January 16, 1976.

8. Carl F. H. Henry, "Abortion: An Evangelical View," in Matthew Avery Sutton, *Jerry Falwell and the Rise of the Religious Right: A Brief History with Documents* (Boston: Bedford/St. Martin's, 2013), 95; Harold Lindsell, *The World, the Flesh, and the Devil* (Minneapolis: World Wide Publications, 1973), 100, 101; Dobson, quoted in Letha Scanzoni, *Sex Is a Parent Affair: Help for Parents in Teaching Their Children about Sex* (Colorado Springs: Regal Books, 1973), 147.

9. Walter Martin, *Abortion: Is It Always Murder?* (Santa Ana, CA: Vision House Publishers, 1977), 5, 43, 42, 44.

10. Seth Dowland, "'Family Values' and the Formation of a Christian Right Agenda," *Church History* 78 (September 2009): 606–31; Robert Case, "Harold O. J. 'Joe' Brown, the Christian Action Council and Me," *Aquila Report*, May 15, 2011, https://www.theaquilareport .com/harold-o-j-joe-brown-the-christian-action-coun cil-and-me/.

CHAPTER SIX

1. For a superb review of the circumstances surrounding the *Green v. Connally* case, see Joseph Crespino, "Civil Rights and the Religious Right," in *Rightward Bound: Making America Conservative in the 1970s*, ed. Bruce J. Schulman and Julian E. Zelizer (Cambridge, MA: Harvard University Press, 2008), 90–105. Crespino correctly identifies *Brown v. Board of Education*, together with *Green v. Connally*, as the catalyst for the Religious Right.

2. Green v. Connally, 330 F. Supp. 1150 (D.D.C.) *aff'd* sub nom. Coit v. Green, 404 U.S. 997 (1971).

3. Green v. Connally, 330 F. Supp. 1150 (D.D.C.) *aff'd* sub nom. Coit v. Green, 404 U.S. 997 (1971).

4. "The Moral Majority" (undated paper, Box 19, Paul M. Weyrich Papers, American Heritage Center, University of Wyoming).

5. Weyrich, quoted in William Martin, *With God on*

Our Side: The Rise of the Religious Right in America (New York: Broadway Books, 1996), 173. As early as February 1979, several months before the formation of an organization by that name, Howard Phillips was using the term "moral majority"; see Phillips to Falwell, February 27, 1979, Evangelist Activism, Box 15, Paul M. Weyrich Papers. According to historian Robert Freedman, "The Supreme Court's banning of public school prayer (1962) and legalization of abortion (1973) outraged many evangelicals and fundamentalists. However, few decided to participate actively in politics as a result." He adds: "Weyrich believes that the Carter administration's policy toward Christian Schools was the turning point." Robert Freedman, "The Religious Right and the Carter Administration," *Historical Journal* 48 (March 2005): 236. Michael Lienesch writes: "The Christian conservative lobbyists were originally concerned with protecting the Christian schools from Internal Revenue Service investigations over the issue of racial imbalance." Michael Lienesch, "Right-Wing Religion: Christian Conservatism as a Political Movement," *Political Science Quarterly* 97 (Autumn 1982): 409. On the importance of schools to the nascent Religious Right, see also J. Charles Park, "Preachers, Politics, and Public Education: A Review of Right-Wing Pressures against Public Schooling in America," *Phi Delta Kappan* 61 (May 1980): 608–12.

6. Falwell, quoted in Martin, *With God on Our Side*, 172.

7. "'Most Unusual': No Time for a Change," *Christianity Today*, December 17, 1971, 34. Bob Jones III insisted that "there was no connection between the enrollment of this one black student and the major threats facing the university." By the way, the call letters for the radio station, WMUU, stand for "world's most unusual university."

8. Dominic Sandbrook, *Mad as Hell: The Crisis of the 1970s and the Rise of the Populist Right* (New York: Anchor Books, 2011), 356.

9. Dobson, quoted in Michael Cromartie, ed., *No Longer Exiles: The Religious New Right in American Politics* (Washington, DC: Ethics and Public Policy Center, 1993), 52; Dan Gilgoff, "Exclusive: Grover Norquist Gives Religious Conservatives Tough Love," *God & Country: On Faith, Politics, and Culture*, June 11, 2009, www.usnews.com/blogs/god-and-country.

10. Elmer L. Rumminger, telephone interview with the author, July 17, 2010.

11. Paul Weyrich, "The Pro-Family Movement," *Conservative Digest* 6 (May-June 1980): 14; Freedman, "Religious Right and the Carter Administration," 238, 240; Wilfred F. Drake, "Tax Status of Private Segregated Schools: The New Revenue Procedure," *William and Mary Law Review* 20 (1979): 463–512; "Jimmy Carter's Betrayal of the Christian Voter," *Conservative Digest*, August 1979, 15; Michael Sean Winters, *God's Right Hand: How Jerry Falwell*

Made God a Republican and Baptized the American Right (San Francisco: HarperOne, 2012), 110; Crespino, "Civil Rights and the Religious Right," 99–100.

12. Weyrich, quoted in Cromartie, *No Longer Exiles*, 26.

CHAPTER SEVEN

1. Billings, quoted in Chuck Stewart, *Gay and Lesbian Issues: A Reference Handbook* (Santa Barbara, CA: ABC-CLIO, 2003), 218.

2. Robert Freedman, "Religious Right and the Carter Administration," *Historical Journal* 48 (March 2005): 240–41, 242; Duane Murray Oldfield, *The Right and the Righteous: The Christian Right Confronts the Republican Party* (Lanham, MD: Rowman & Littlefield, 1996), 100.

3. Robert H. DuVall, president, American Council of Christian Churches, news release, May 17, 1971, Valley Forge, PA; Robert Eels and Bartell Nyberg, *Lonely Walk: The Life of Senator Mark Hatfield* (Chappaqua, NY: Christian Herald Books, 1979), 95; Lon Fendall, *Stand Alone or Come Home: Mark Hatfield as an Evangelical and a Progressive* (Newberg, OR: Barclay, 2008), 155–58. Hatfield maintained his opposition to abortion throughout his life, but he also supported Planned Parenthood, especially its sex education and contraception efforts, and he consistently linked a "pro-life" position with opposition to capital punishment, support for gun control, and anti-

poverty programs; see Mark O. Hatfield, with Diane N. Solomon, *Against the Grain: Reflections of a Rebel Republican* (Ashland, OR: White Cloud, 2001), 89–92.

4. Harold O. J. Brown, "The Passivity of American Christians," *Christianity Today*, January 16, 1976.

5. Freedman, "Religious Right and the Carter Administration," 243.

6. Douglas E. Kneeland, "Clark Defeat in Iowa Laid to Abortion Issue," *New York Times*, November 13, 1978; Daniel K. Williams, *God's Own Party: The Making of the Christian Right* (New York: Oxford University Press, 2010), 154; Dick Clark, interview with Bruce Morton, CBS News, November 13, 1978. See also Hedrick Smith, "A Pattern of Stability: With Incumbents Faring Well, Results Indicate That Fears of Voter Revolt Were Exaggerated," *New York Times*, November 8, 1978. Allegations later emerged that the white government of South Africa may have illegally contributed money toward Clark's defeat because of his strong stand against apartheid. Wendell Rawls Jr., "South African Role in Iowa Voting Charged," *New York Times*, March 22, 1979.

7. "Religion at the Polls: Strength and Conflict," *Christianity Today*, December 1, 1978, 40–41.

8. Weyrich to Hales, December 31, 1978, Box 3, Paul M. Weyrich Papers, American Heritage Center, University of Wyoming.

9. Francis A. Schaeffer, quoted in Jean Garton, "25th

Anniversary of the Roe v. Wade Case," *National Right to Life News* (newsletter), September 28, 1998; Frank Schaeffer, *Crazy for God: How I Grew Up as One of the Elect, Helped Found the Religious Right, and Lived to Take All (or Almost All) of It Back* (New York: Carroll & Graf, 2007), 293; Frank Schaeffer, conversation with the author, April 8, 2019. Frank Schaeffer, who regards "abortion as an unmitigated tragedy," writes: "Evangelicals weren't politicized (at least in the current meaning of the word) until after *Roe v. Wade* and after Dad, Koop, and I stirred them up over the issue of abortion." Schaeffer, *Crazy for God*, 345.

10. Regarding Carter's position on abortion, see Randall Balmer, *Redeemer: The Life of Jimmy Carter* (New York: Basic Books, 2014), 96–98.

CHAPTER EIGHT

1. James Robison, "Remembering Reagan," *James Robison: A Weekly Commentary*, June 8, 2004, http://archives.jamesrobison.net/columns/060804.htm. I should disclose that I was a congressional intern for John B. Anderson in the House Republican Caucus during the summer of 1975; Anderson was chair of the caucus. He was also a member of the board of trustees at my undergraduate institution: Trinity College, Deerfield, Illinois.

2. News Release [text of Reagan's address to the Round-table, National Affairs Briefing, Dallas, Texas], August 22, 1980, folder "Tour Files—Dallas, Texas—8/21-22/1980," Box 144, Reagan, Ronald: 1980 Campaign Papers, 1965–80, Edwin Meese Files, Ronald Reagan Library.

3. News Release, August 22, 1980, Reagan Library.

4. Weyrich, quoted in Katherine Stewart, *The Power Worshippers: Inside the Dangerous Rise of Religious Nationalism* (New York: Bloomsbury, 2020), 102; Paul Weyrich, "Reagan Edgy with Evangelicals," August 25, 1980, Editorials—Curmudgeon Column, 1980, Box 17, Paul M. Weyrich Papers, American Heritage Center, University of Wyoming.

5. Cal Thomas and Ed Dobson, *Blinded by Might: Can the Religious Right Save America?* (Grand Rapids: Zondervan, 1999), 16.

CHAPTER NINE

1. Lou Cannon, *President Reagan: The Role of a Lifetime* (New York: Simon & Schuster, 1991), 459; Glenn H. Utter and John Woodrow Storey, *The Religious Right: A Reference Handbook*, 2nd ed. (Santa Barbara, CA: ABC-CLIO, 2001), s.v. "Robert J. Billings." Not all evangelical schools were segregated—by no means. When a government official asked Oral Roberts about the racial policies at Oral Roberts University, Roberts replied, "whether we

get any federal funds or not, we'll be international, interdenominational and interracial." Oral Roberts, "God Doesn't Look at Skin Color" (chapel address at Oral Roberts University, September 26, 1989, Chapel Audio & Transcripts, Oral Roberts University Collection). In 1956, Roberts, who was himself part Cherokee, declared, "My ministry is for all people of all churches and all races." Daniel D. Isgrigg, "Healing for All Races: Oral Roberts' Legacy of Racial Reconciliation in a Divided City," *Spiritus: ORU Journal of Theology* 4 (2019): 233.

2. Jon Meacham, "The South's Fight for White Supremacy," *New York Times*, August 23, 2020. On government policies that disadvantaged African Americans, see Richard Rothstein, *The Color of Law: A Forgotten History of How Our Government Segregated America* (New York: Norton, 2017). On the persistence of the mythologies underlying white supremacy, see Richard T. Hughes, *Myths America Lives By: White Supremacy and the Stories That Give Us Meaning* (Chicago and Urbana: University of Illinois Press, 2018).

3. On Carter vanquishing the Democratic Party's legacy of racism, see Jonathan Alter, *His Very Best: Jimmy Carter, A Life* (New York: Simon & Schuster, 2020), 237.

4. Daniel S. Lucks, *Reconsidering Reagan: Racism, Republicans, and the Road to Trump* (Boston: Beacon, 2020), 72–73.

5. Reagan, quoted in Lucks, *Reconsidering Reagan*, 86; Tim Naftali, "Ronald Reagan's Long-Hidden Racist Conversation with Richard Nixon," *Atlantic*, July 30, 2019.

6. Joseph Crespino, "Civil Rights and the Religious Right," in *Rightward Bound: Making America Conservative in the 1970s*, ed. Bruce J. Schulman and Julian E. Zelizer (Cambridge, MA: Harvard University Press, 2008), 104.

7. Douglas E. Kneeland, "Reagan Campaigns at Mississippi Fair," *New York Times*, August 4, 1980; Lucks, *Reconsidering Reagan*, 145. Although the Reagan-Bush campaign repudiated support of the Ku Klux Klan, a month following Reagan's appearance in Philadelphia the campaign received a telegram from the grand wizard of the Knights of the Ku Klux Klan, Tuscumbia, Alabama, promising that if Reagan continued his support for "anti white discrimination" and a range of issues, Reagan "will receive the support of our membership as well as the majority of all Americans." Mailgram, Don Black, September 3, 1980, folder "Ku Klux Klan," Box 132, Reagan, Ronald: 1980 Campaign Papers, 1965–80, Edwin Meese files, Ronald Reagan Library.

8. Lucks, *Reconsidering Reagan*, 179–83.

9. Falwell, quoted in Max Blumenthal, "Agent of Intolerance," *Nation*, May 29, 2007; Falwell, quoted in Lucks, *Reconsidering Reagan*, 140; William R. Goodman Jr. and

James J. H. Price, *Jerry Falwell: An Unauthorized Biography* (Lynchburg, VA: Paris & Assoc., 1981), 118. Frank Schaeffer, Francis A. Schaeffer's son, remembered Falwell as an "unreconstructed bigot." Frank Schaeffer, *Crazy for God: How I Grew Up as One of the Elect, Helped Found the Religious Right, and Lived to Take All (or Almost All) of It Back* (New York: Carroll & Graf, 2007), 315.

10. Jerry Falwell, "Ministers and Marches," in Matthew Avery Sutton, *Jerry Falwell and the Religious Right: A Brief History with Documents* (New York: St. Martin's, 2012), 59, 60; Falwell, quoted in Blumenthal, "Agent of Intolerance." Blumenthal misstates the year Falwell delivered the sermon, but he correctly writes, "Indeed, it was race—not abortion or the attendant suite of so-called 'values' issues—that propelled Falwell and his evangelical allies into political activism."

11. LaHaye to Hudson T. Armerding [president of Wheaton College], May 23, 1968, Wheaton College Archives and Special Collections.

12. Weyrich, quoted in Dudley Clendinen, "Rev. Falwell Inspires Evangelical Vote," *New York Times*, August 20, 1980, B22.

13. Max Blumenthal, "Justice Sunday Preachers," *Nation*, April 26, 2005; Randall Balmer, "The Other Louisianan with a Tawdry History of Speaking to Racist Groups," History News Network, January 14, 2015,

http://ww.hnn.us/article/158175; "a retrograde species of humanity" quoted in Heidi Beirich and Kevin Hicks, "White Nationalism in America," in *Hate Crimes*, ed. Barbara Perry et al., 5 vols. (Westport, CT: Praeger, 2009), 1:110.

14. Michelle Goldberg, "The White Supremacy Caucus," *New York Times*, December 11, 2017. I have written extensively about Moore and his Ten Commandments caper; see Randall Balmer, *Thy Kingdom Come: How the Religious Right Distorts the Faith and Threatens America* (New York: Basic Books, 2006), chap. 2; Balmer, "I Know Roy Moore. He's Always Been a Con Artist," *Washington Post*, November 19, 2017.

15. Stevens, quoted in S. V. Date, "Republicans Jostling for 2024 Presidential Bids Could Face Yet Another Donald Trump," *HuffPost*, August 24, 2020, https://www.huffpost.com/entry/trump-jr-dynasty_n_5f3ef43ac5b697824f965a31.

16. Randall Balmer, "Under Trump, Evangelicals Show Their True Racist Colors," *Los Angeles Times*, August 23, 2017.

17. Falwell, quoted in Blumenthal, "Agent of Intolerance."

18. Matthew 12:25 (KJV).

19. John Wagner, "'Pro-family Leaders' Ask House GOP Leader to Reinstate Rep. King's Committee Memberships," *Washington Post*, February 12, 2019; Trip Ga-

briel, "A Timeline of Steve King's Racist Remarks and Divisive Actions," *New York Times*, January 15, 2019; Justin Miller, "Steve King Has a Friend in Texas Congressman Louie Gohmert," *Texas Observer*, January 18, 2019. On Gohmert's ties to the Religious Right, see Balmer, *Thy Kingdom Come*, 37.

20. Jeffress, quoted in Michael J. Mooney, "The Pastor and the President," *Texas Monthly*, August 2019; Jerry Falwell Jr., quoted in Sarah Pulliam Bailey, "'Their Dream President': Trump Just Gave White Evangelicals a Big Boost," *Washington Post*, March 4, 2017; Ralph Reed, "Trump Is Reviving America's Christian Heritage," *AllOnGeorgia*, January 7, 2020, https://allongeorgia.com /georgia-opinions/column-trump-is-reviving-americas -christian-heritage/; Elana Schor and Emily Swanson, "Poll: White Evangelicals Distinct on Abortion, LGBT Policy," Associated Press, January 2, 2020, https://ap news.com/8d3eb99934accc2ad795aca018329 0a7.

21. Daniel K. Williams, *Defenders of the Unborn: The Pro-Life Movement before* Roe v. Wade (New York: Oxford University Press, 2016).

POSTSCRIPT

1. Joseph Crespino, "Civil Rights and the Religious Right," in *Rightward Bound: Making America Conservative in the 1970s*, ed. Bruce J. Schulman and Julian E.

Zelizer (Cambridge, MA: Harvard University Press, 2008), 104-5.

2. Regarding the Bob Jones University case, see Olatunde C. Johnson, "The Story of *Bob Jones University v. United States* (1983): Race, Religion, and Congress' Extraordinary Acquiescence," in *Statutory Interpretation Stories*, ed. William Eskridge, Philip P. Frickey, and Elizabeth Garrett (New York: Foundation Press, 2010), 126-65.

Suggestions for Further Reading

Balmer, Randall. *Redeemer: The Life of Jimmy Carter*. New York: Basic Books, 2014.

Cannon, Mae Elise, et al. *Forgive Us: Confessions of a Compromised Faith*. Grand Rapids: Zondervan, 2014.

Collins, John. *What Are Biblical Values? What the Bible Says on Key Ethical Issues*. New Haven: Yale University Press, 2019.

Cromartie, Michael, ed. *No Longer Exiles: The Religious New Right in American Politics*. Washington, DC: Ethics and Public Policy Center, 1993.

Denker, Angela. *Red State Christian: Understanding the Voters Who Elected Donald Trump*. Minneapolis: Fortress, 2019.

Du Mez, Kristen Kobes. *Jesus and John Wayne: How White Evangelicals Corrupted a Faith and Fractured a Nation*. New York: Liveright, 2020.

Fea, John. *Believe Me: The Evangelical Road to Donald Trump*. Grand Rapids: Eerdmans, 2020.

Gilgoff, Dan. *The Jesus Machine: How James Dobson, Fo-*

cus on the Family, and Evangelical America Are Winning the Culture War. New York: St. Martin's, 2007.

Glaude, Eddie S., Jr. Democracy in Black: How Race Still Enslaves the American Soul. New York: Crown, 2017.

Harper, Lisa Sharon. Evangelical Does Not Equal Republican or Democrat. Foreword by John M. Perkins. New York: New Press, 2008.

———. The Very Good Gospel: How Everything Wrong Can Be Made Right. Foreword by Walter Brueggemann. Colorado Springs: WaterBrook & Multnomah, 2016.

Ingersoll, Julie J. Building God's Kingdom: Inside the World of Christian Reconstruction. New York: Oxford University Press, 2015.

Jennings, Willie James. The Christian Imagination: Theology and the Origins of Race. New Haven: Yale University Press, 2011.

Jones, Robert P. White Too Long: The Legacy of White Supremacy in American Christianity. New York: Simon & Schuster, 2020.

Keddie, Tony. Republican Jesus: How the Right Has Rewritten the Gospels. Berkeley: University of California Press, 2020.

Lucks, Daniel S. *Reconsidering Reagan: Racism, Republicans, and the Road to Trump*. Boston: Beacon, 2020.

Martin, Walter. *Abortion: Is It Always Murder?* Santa Ana, CA: Vision House, 1977.

Martin, William. *With God on Our Side: The Rise of the Religious Right in America*. New York: Broadway Books, 1996.

Moore, Andrew S., ed. *Evangelicals and Presidential Politics: From Jimmy Carter to Donald Trump*. Baton Rouge: Louisiana State University Press, 2021.

Nelson, Anne. *Shadow Network: Media, Money, and the Secret Hub of the Radical Right*. New York: Bloomsbury, 2019.

Posner, Sarah. *Unholy: Why White Evangelicals Worship at the Altar of Donald Trump*. New York: Random House, 2020.

Schaeffer, Frank. *Crazy for God: How I Grew Up as One of the Elect, Helped Found the Religious Right, and Lived to Take All (or Almost All) of It Back*. New York: Carroll & Graf, 2007.

Schulman, Bruce J., and Julian E. Zelizer, eds. *Rightward Bound: Making America Conservative in the 1970s*. Cambridge: Harvard University Press, 2008.

Sider, Ronald J., ed. *The Spiritual Danger of Donald*

Trump: 30 Evangelical Christians on Justice, Truth, and Moral Integrity. Eugene, OR: Cascade Books, 2020.

Stevens, Stuart. *It Was All a Lie: How the Republican Party Became Donald Trump.* New York: Alfred A. Knopf, 2020.

Stewart, Katherine. *The Power Worshippers: Inside the Dangerous Rise of Religious Nationalism.* New York: Bloomsbury, 2020.

Stout, Jeffrey. *Democracy and Tradition.* Rev. ed. Princeton: Princeton University Press, 2004.

Sutton, Matthew Avery. *American Apocalypse: A History of Modern Evangelicalism.* Cambridge, MA: Harvard University Press, 2014.

Swartz, David R. *Moral Minority: The Evangelical Left in an Age of Conservatism.* Philadelphia: University of Pennsylvania Press, 2012.

Thomas, Cal, and Ed Dobson. *Blinded by Might: Can the Religious Right Save America?* Grand Rapids: Zondervan, 1999.

West, Cornel. *Race Matters.* Boston: Beacon, 2017.

Whitehead, Andrew L., and Samuel L. Perry. *Taking America Back for God: Christian Nationalism in the United States.* New York: Oxford University Press, 2020.

Williams, Daniel K. *Defenders of the Unborn: The Pro-Life Movement before* Roe v. Wade. New York: Oxford University Press, 2016.

———. *God's Own Party: The Making of the Christian Right.* New York: Oxford University Press, 2012.

Winters, Michael Sean. *God's Right Hand: How Jerry Falwell Made God a Republican and Baptized the American Right.* San Francisco: HarperOne, 2012.

Ziegler, Mary. *Abortion and the Law in America: Roe v. Wade to the Present.* Cambridge: Cambridge University Press, 2020.

Index

About the Author

Before earning the PhD from Princeton University, Randall Balmer graduated from Trinity College and Trinity Evangelical Divinity School. He was a professor of American religious history at Columbia University for twenty-seven years before moving to Dartmouth College in 2012, where he is the John Phillips Professor in Religion, the oldest endowed professorship at the college. He is the author of more than a dozen books, including *Evangelicalism in America* and *Redeemer: The Life of Jimmy Carter*. His second book, *Mine Eyes Have Seen the Glory: A Journey into the Evangelical Subculture in America*, now in its fifth edition, was made into a three-part series for PBS. Dr. Balmer was nominated for an Emmy for writing and hosting that series. His commentaries have appeared in newspapers around the country, including the *Los Angeles Times*, the *Washington Post*, the *Des Moines Register*, *Stars and Stripes*, and the *Santa Fe New Mexican*. He was ordained an Episcopal priest in 2006. He and his wife, Catharine Randall, reside in Vermont and New Mexico.